Refugees

THE WASHINGTON PAPERS

... intended to meet the need for an authoritative, yet prompt, public appraisal of the major developments in world affairs.

Series Editors: Walter Laqueur; Amos A. Jordan

Associate Editors: William J. Taylor, Jr.; Thomas Bleha

Executive Editor: Jean C. Newsom

Managing Editor: Nancy B. Eddy

Editorial Assistant: Christine L. Zibas

President, CSIS: Amos A. Jordan

MANUSCRIPT SUBMISSION

The Washington Papers and Praeger Publishers welcome inquiries concerning manuscript submissions. Please include with your inquiry a curriculum vitae, synopsis, table of contents, and estimated manuscript length. Manuscripts must be between 120–200 double-spaced typed pages. All submissions will be peer reviewed. Submissions to *The Washington Papers* should be sent to *The Washington Papers*; The Center for Strategic and International Studies; 1800 K Street NW; Suite 400; Washington, DC 20006. Book proposals should be sent to Praeger Publishers; One Madison Avenue; New York NY 10010.

Refugees

Extended Exile

W. R. Smyser

Foreword by Leo Cherne

Published with The Center for
Strategic and International Studies
Washington, D.C.

PRAEGER

New York
Westport, Connecticut
London

Library of Congress Cataloging-in-Publication Data

Smyser, W. R., 1931–
  Refugees : extended exile.

  (The Washington papers, ISSN 0278-937X ; 129)
  "Published with the Center for Strategic and
International Studies, Washington, D.C."
  "Praeger special studies. Praeger scientific."
  Bibliography: p.
  Includes index.
  1. Refugees. I. Title. II. Series.
HV640.S66 1988   362.8'7   87-20957
ISBN 0-275-92877-2 (alk. paper)
ISBN 0-275-92878-0 (pbk. : alk. paper)

Library of Congress Catalog Card Number: 87-20957
ISBN: 0-275-92877-2 cloth
        0-275-92878-0 paper

First published in 1987

Praeger Publishers, One Madison Avenue, New York, NY 10010
A division of Greenwood Press, Inc.

Printed in the United States of America

The paper used in this book complies with the Permanent
Paper Standard issued by the National Information Standards
Organization (Z39.48-1984).

10 9 8 7 6 5 4 3 2 1

Contents

Foreword

The past decade has seen a quantum leap in the magnitude, complexity, and intractability of refugee crises and emergencies around the world. The institutions – international, national, and private – that have come into being since World Wars I and II have been strained to the maximum by these challenges. Indeed, it is not inappropriate to ask if these institutional structures in place today can hold, or whether they risk being washed away by the flood tides of refugees, the homeless, the desperate, the persecuted, the sick, and the starving.

What is so compelling in W. R. Smyser's work is its placing of today's refugee problem in the broader historical context of the post World War I and World War II periods. We learn again, as if for the first time, that the past decade has indeed been unique and that the institutions carefully and painstakingly built up since 1918 could never have imagined the size and complexity of the world refugee situation we face as the final decade of the twentieth century approaches.

This should not be a source of despair, however, but rather for hope that the ingenuity and compassionate sides of human nature are capable of rising to the occasion when put to the test. Dick Smyser goes to some pains, and properly so, to describe the massive population movements following the First World War and how concerned persons of good will were able to establish principles and create institutions that managed, at least in part, to limit the suffering of the refugees. These efforts, alas, could not prevent, for example, the pitiless massacre of hundreds of thousands of Armenians. And, indeed, the whole structure, principles and all, was washed away by the tidal wave of Nazi terror and genocide. World War II and the fanatical final solution of Hitler's Reich represent momentous failures for persons of good will everywhere and should stand as mute testimony of the darkest sides of humanity that lurk beneath the veneer of civilization.

The post World War II period, as this book so well describes, saw a truly massive undertaking to resettle the millions of displaced persons, surviving victims of that conflict. It was not until the early 1960s, a full 15 years after the end of hostilities, that the final chapter of the displaced persons program in Europe could be written. And while it was being written, new refugee populations were emerging, from behind the iron curtain and from the areas of the world undergoing the sudden rush to independence and a throwing off of the colonial yoke.

The post World War II period, as this book so well describes, saw a truly massive undertaking to resettle the millions of displaced persons, surviving victims of that conflict. It was not until the early 1960s, a full 15 years after the end of hostilities, that the final chapter of the displaced persons program in Europe could be written. And while it was being written, new refugee populations were emerging, from behind the iron curtain and from the areas of the world undergoing the sudden rush to independence and a throwing off of the colonial yoke.

New covenants, new institutions, and new structures were created to meet these new challenges, and by and large they have operated with success. The International Refugee Organization, the United Nations High Commissioner for

Refugees, the convention and the protocol are all post World War II creations in response to new crises and new challenges. With the exception of the Palestinian refugees, which stand as a signal warning of what can result from a failure of international diplomacy, the present structures have stood the test of time.

As the author points out, the sovereign nations of Africa and Latin America have, in their separate and unique ways, developed regional means of cooperation and understanding regarding refugee flows between their respective borders and the asylum procedures to be observed. At the same time, international agencies such as the UNHCR, the International Committee for the Red Cross, and the Intergovernmental Committee for Migration, as well as a burgeoning number of private voluntary agencies committed to assisting refugees, have created a stronger international response mechanism and infrastructure to meet new crises.

But, if there is a watershed year that has changed the scope, dimension, and complexity of refugee emergencies it is 1979–1980. During this period, the phenomenon of Vietnamese boat people fleeing persecution by the hundreds of thousands was followed immediately by the flight of more than 2 million Afghans following the Soviet invasion of their country. These, in turn, were followed by the tragedy of Cambodia, as hollow-eyed survivors of Pol Pot's "social experiments" staggered into Thailand by the thousands, only, in too many cases, to die. In short order came the Mariel Cubans, with thousands taking the opportunity to flee Castro's Cuba by boat, the plight of fewer but no less compelling numbers of Haitians, Salvadorans, Guatemalans, and Nicaraguans. Then, nature, political manipulation, and ruthless military action combined to provoke the exodus of hundreds of thousands of Ethiopians, first to Somalia and Djibouti and then to the Sudan.

No decade has known such concentrated refugee activity of such magnitude and for so sustained a period. Dick Smyser describes it all, and does it well, raising the new elements of these movements that call for new responses,

ix

new approaches, and new intiatives. The phenomenom of refugees in the Third World, the intractability of their plight, the threats worldwide to the principles of first asylum, the strengths and weaknesses of the classic "solutions" to refugee movements — voluntary repatriation, settlement in place, and resettlement in third countries — are all analyzed here. Although he does not use the term, the concept of "compassion fatigue" is alluded to, as is the growing xenophobia of the industrialized countries of Europe and the West regarding asylum seekers from the less developed world.

There are no easy answers or a magic wand for today's refugee crises. There are probably few if any reliable ways to anticipate the crises of the future. But this book demonstrates beyond the shadow of a doubt is that, when properly energized, the international community can respond to even the most taxing crises with determination, imagination, vigor, and compassion. This is the bright side of the analysis. The dark side is what can result if the response is found wanting. Recent history points to a regrettable number of such instances as well — none more telling that the holocaust of World War II and the on-going tragedy of the Palestinian refugees.

What the outcome will be, no one can know. However, thanks to the existence of works such as this, we are compelled to know our recent past and present. Knowing these can, at least in part, help guide us in the future. For this, as for his many years of distinguished public service, we can only be deeply grateful to Dick Smyser. This is a superior piece of scholarship and a provocative, timely, and challenging work.

Leo Cherne
Chairman
International Rescue Committee

About the Author

W. R. Smyser was United Nations deputy high commissioner for refugees from 1981 to 1986. Before then, he served as assistant director and director of the U.S. State Department Bureau for Refugee Programs. He has visited more than three dozen countries to inspect or negotiate refugee programs. He has served in the U.S. Foreign Service and at the National Security Council and held fellowships at Harvard University and the Georgetown University Center for Strategic and International Studies. He has written several books and articles, including "Refugees: The Never-Ending Story," in the fall 1985 issue of *Foreign Affairs*. He holds a Ph.D. from George Washington University.

Preface

At the extreme eastern edge of the Sudan lies a border crossing named Tuk el Baab. I went there in December 1984 to see for myself how best to help starving refugees then streaming into Sudan on the dirt trails from Tigre and Eritrea in Ethiopia.

In the dust and the flat afternoon light, at first I could only make out the outline of some rocky border hills and of hundreds of dry shrubs at their base. As I came closer, I noticed that under each shrub, only slightly sheltered from the direct sun during the day, sat or lay small groups of refugees. Already preparing for the night, they were wrapping themselves in the few available blankets and in what little clothing remained to them. Because the stone and the soil would retain the warmth of the day longer than the air, they were placing their youngest children in hollows that they had dug as close as possible to the rocks.

I went to the emergency feeding shelter, one of those flat-topped beige tents that seem to be a part of every relief operation. Sudanese, European, and American nutritionists were working around the clock to save the lives of emaciated adults and of children so thin one could barely detect flesh. As I came out, I saw a man whose 12-year-old son had just died. He had washed the boy's body ceremonially as best he could and, following Muslim tradition, was just wrapping him in a white shroud.

After six years of refugee work, such are the moments, the faces, and the people that are etched into my memory: the mute despair of Khmer refugees at Khao I Dang in eastern Thailand, unsure whether any country would accept them and their families, powerless to control their future, afraid to return home, and able only to plead with tired voices and anxious eyes; the three shrines – Catholic, Protestant, and Buddhist – gleaming white on a peak of Pulau Bidong island off the coast of Malaysia; the deep rumble of a thousand throats when, speaking to Afghan refugees in a camp near Peshawar in western Pakistan, I spoke of our hope to see them return home one day; the drive, energy, and enthusiasm of children at Mishamo settlement in Tanzania, helping to prepare the soil by tilling with the simplest of tools, as well as the proud bearing of the women returning to Arua in northern Uganda after years of refuge in Zaire.

In this brief survey I will attempt to cover a number of basic elements of the current global refugee problem. I will summarize the origin and the state of refugee law and assistance, delineate the vast structure that has been established to receive, to help, and to transport refugees, describe the long parade of refugees themselves, and set out the most urgent problems. I cannot help but list a daunting array of statistics, but I hope that those who read the book will try to remember that a book about refugees is fundamentally a book about people. Refugees are people – individuals, families, or whole nations – who have fled danger to accept uncertainty. Their lives are dominated by extremes of fear and hope that those in comfortable, free, and settled societies often cannot comprehend.

I will attempt to describe the situations of refugees virtually everywhere in the world, including those who flee from one continent to another. I will not, however, cover the Palestinian refugees in the Middle East. Theirs is also an extended exile, and a longer one than others, but those refugees are not within my area of experience and expertise.

To keep the book within reasonable limits, I have not written at length about any particular refugee crisis or about any particular aspect of the global refugee problem. Instead, I have given a general survey of the field for those who wish to examine the principal issues. For the benefit of those who want to use this book as a springboard for more detailed study, I have used the endnotes to cite some of the body of literature being produced by the small but growing body of academic and professional experts on refugee and migration matters. On occasion, I have drawn on my own knowledge, experience, and impressions.

In the final chapter I have taken the liberty of making some recommendations. I had made a number of similar recommendations while in office.[1] I have now put them into more detail than I did then and have written with greater urgency on some issues that I find increasingly worrisome.

This book could not have been written without a thoughtful and generous grant from the Ford Foundation, which I hereby gratefully acknowledge. I would also like to acknowledge all the other work that the Foundation has done over the years to support protection of, assistance to, and research about refugees. I particularly want to thank Frank Thomas, Susan Berresford, Enid Schoettle, and Paul Balaran for their encouragement and support.

I want to express my thanks to other organizations that have helped me in the research and to many persons within those organizations: the Refugee Policy Group, the U.S. Committee on Refugees, the Refugee Documentation Center, InterAction, and many voluntary agencies. I also want to thank the UN High Commissioner for Refugees, Jean-Pierre Hocké, for giving me access to his offices to bring my research up-to-date, as well as one of his predecessors, Prince Sadruddin Aga Khan, for his interest.

I particularly wish to express my thanks to former High Commissioner Poul Hartling, who invited me to work with him and who gave me the opportunity to see what is written about here. I have also had the privilege of consulting many friends and former colleagues at the office of the UN High Commissioner for Refugees, at the U.S. Department of State, and with other governments and organizations. If this book has merit, it is thanks to many efforts to enlighten me and provide a sounding board for my thoughts. I accept full responsibility for any defects and for my opinions and recommendations.

Beyond these acknowledgments, however, I must also cite at least some of the others whom I came to know, persons who contributed to my education and thought in ways that they and I may not have fully realized at the time: the Belgian nun of the Franciscan Sisters who escorted me late at night in a driving rainstorm around the hospital in Zaire where she had served for more than 20 years and where she was then helping hundreds of persons who had just fled across the border from Angola; the Irish woman who, as chief of the High Commissioner's office in Juba, Sudan, twice declined my invitation for her to leave her post in the face of the advancing civil war; the Japanese whom I met, far from family and friends, serving with great dedication at Quetta in Pakistan; finally, two particular Americans – one a nutritionist whom I saw several times during my field visits in the most rigorous crisis areas, another a former prisoner of the Viet Cong who chose to go back to Southeast Asia to help Vietnamese refugees, countrymen of those who had held him captive.

It is from such experiences, and from such recollections, that the dedication of this book must come: To the refugees of the world, and to those who serve them in the field.

Refugees

Introduction

Our century has sometimes been called the "Century of the Refugee." It has earned that dubious honor although refugees certainly do not constitute a new phenomenon. Never in history, however, have there been so many refugees from so many countries. Never has world consciousness about the plight of refugees been as high as it is now. And never have so many remained as long in the kind of suspended animation that refugee status now all too often has come to mean.

The global refugee problem is at an important juncture. In the past, refugees were a temporary phenomenon. They came and went, either returning home, settling where they were, or moving on to yet another country where they could resettle. Now, however, they come and stay. For almost 10 years, the number of refugees throughout the world has been constant at about 10 to 12 million persons. Even though some groups have declined in number, others have become larger. They have constituted a significant drain on resources, often for the poorest countries. They represent a tragic phenomenon of displacement, persons who cannot work and who cannot take care of many of their own basic needs, children who live out their lives in camps with little promise for a stable future.

1

There is growing evidence that the world is tiring of this persistent emergency. Some refugee problems, like those of Southeast Asia, have passed from the center of world attention and are now dangerously near neglect. Many asylum countries are increasingly concerned that they may be left with a long-term refugee presence and are pulling up the welcome mat.

Countries that have been the pillars of refugee protection and assistance now seem to be turning xenophobic when faced with new and uncontrolled numbers of arrivals. The distinctions between refugees and migrants are becoming confused. Some migrants appear to be abusing the rights intended for refugees. The nature of refugee problems has changed so much that we must review some of our ways of dealing with it.

The University of Pennsylvania has a motto that is appropriate to the present situation: *Leges sine Moribus Vanae* – "Laws without customs are vain." The structure of refugee law and care, which has been generously assembled since the dawn of our culture and particularly in the twentieth century, cannot remain in place if it is abandoned by political and popular opinion. If the people of the world decide that they no longer wish to receive and help refugees, all the international conventions and organizations will be rendered useless and will prove unequal to the task of saving even a single life. That is a danger that must be averted.

Refugees, however, are not like actors. They cannot appear when we are ready and disappear when we are tired. Their coming and their staying are dictated not by their choice but by their need. They are the victims of circumstances that they did not desire or create. The world must either solve the problems that create the refugees – and that keep creating them – or it must solve the problems of the refugees themselves.

1

The Origins

There have always been refugees, because there have always been those who could not accept the society or the state in which they lived and those whom society or states could not accept. Such persons have often chosen to go into exile, or have been sent. Many creative or political personalities have become refugees. The list includes such diverse persons as Thomas Becket, Marlene Dietrich, Albert Einstein, Victor Hugo, Vladimir Lenin, Sun Yat-sen, and Richard Wagner. Sometimes entire peoples have chosen or been compelled to flee, whether the Jews and Muslims from Spain or the Huguenots from France.

In the twentieth century, the number of refugees has multiplied beyond all historical precedent. Some refugee departures have turned into great migrations, like that of the Germans from Eastern Europe and Eastern Germany into the Federal Republic of Germany or that of the Muslims from India into Pakistan and the Hindus from Pakistan into India. Although no statistics are fully reliable, the number of refugees in this century already exceeds 60 million, a staggering mass larger than the population of most of the countries of the world. It is ironic and depressing that such a phenomenon should be so widespread during an era that we often regard as the pinnacle of civilization.

The nature and power of the modern state and of modern conflict have helped generate these vast numbers of refugees. States are now better organized and equipped than ever before to decide and to enforce how their citizens behave. Within their borders, they can impose their laws and decrees more effectively. They can demand absolute obedience and can exact absolute penalties. They can record and recall what their citizens have done or not done. Moreover, the many modern states that claim a revolutionary mission also insist on prescribing the terms under which their citizens must participate in that revolution and the degree to which they are required to do so. Those who are not prepared to abide by these prescriptions have little choice but to leave.

The homogeneous character of many populations reinforces the compulsion for unanimity. The nation-state, a phenomenon that developed in Europe during the nineteenth century and has become widespread during the twentieth, all too often believes that it can insist on unanimity because its people are supposedly of one kind and should, therefore, logically be of one persuasion. But even people sharing an ethnic origin do not always agree. Furthermore, where such a nation-state does not exist, the pressures for separate national or tribal autonomy or independence may lead to surreptitious resistance, terrorist activity, or insurrection, sometimes supported or even directed from abroad. All these may in turn lead to violent government repression.

The nature of conflict has also changed during this century. War, whether civil or international, can be conducted by more pervasive and more powerful means. Armed forces, whether security, constabulary, or regular military forces, can kill or maim more persons than ever before. People cannot hope to insulate themselves from violence, whether the instruments of that violence are in the hands of government forces, rebel forces, or contending national armies. When a conflict approaches their homes, they must leave.

The Tradition of Refugee Protection

These contemporary phenomena became brutally evident during and immediately after World War I in the chaos of the postwar period and particularly in the collapse of the Russian imperial regime and the dismemberment of the Austrian and Ottoman empires. One and a half million Russians fled several successive revolutions, the long resistance wars, and the destruction of the society they had known. More than one-half million persons, mainly Armenians but also Greeks and Assyrians, fled from Ottoman territories as the authority of the empire crumbled. Many who had lived quietly and even prosperously in the cosmopolitan kaleidoscope of the Austro-Hungarian empire suddenly found themselves to be isolated minorities in one of the fiercely nationalist successor states. Refugees, produced almost casually by the rearrangement of European borders, went in all directions. Hungarians fled Romania. Serbs fled Hungary. Refugees poured into Western Europe and, to a lesser degree, into the Middle East.[2]

Europe, still exhausted from the war, was unable to receive or to help the new arrivals. National authorities were uncertain even whether to admit the refugees and, if they were admitted, whether to treat them as legitimate immigrants, illegal aliens, or temporary visitors. Few resources could be placed at their disposal. Only a handful of persons understood the dimensions of the tragedy and the urgency of the needs. The refugees shuffled on in confusion and disarray, searching for relatives, friends, fellow nationals, churches, or charitable institutions that could help. Those who tried to help often found that their resources could not begin to match the requirements of the situation.

The representatives of a group of charitable organizations met in Geneva, Switzerland in February 1921 to find a common answer to the problem. Through the president of the International Red Cross, they asked the League of Nations to appoint a commissioner to guide and coordinate their efforts. The League appointed Dr. Fridtjof Nansen, a distinguished Norwegian explorer and humanitarian, to be "High Commissioner on behalf of the League" to deal with refugee matters. He was instructed to determine the legal status of the refugees and to find a permanent solution for them, either by repatriation, integration into the countries in which they had found asylum, or resettlement to other countries where they might wish to go and where they might be welcome. His task was assumed to be temporary.[3]

During the years to follow, the High Commissioner addressed the whole range of refugee problems. Those included protection and relief for the Russian, Armenian, Assyrian, and other refugee groups as well as the exchange of populations between Greece and Turkey. He persuaded the governments of the asylum countries to issue a new document, known as the "Nansen Passport," to identify the new arrivals and to give them a definite status. When his commission expired in 1929, it was followed by the creation of the International Nansen Office for Refugees, established with the stipulation that it, too, was temporary and was to cease its functions no later than December 31, 1938.

Even as refugees were being received and assisted, the Western states attempted to find some common position on the status and the rights of the new arrivals. They came to several agreements in 1922, 1924, and 1926 regarding the Russian and Armenian refugees. In 1928 they signed an accord governing identity documents for these refugees as well as for several other groups.[4]

The Nansen Office could not finish its work by 1938 as expected. With the disruption caused by the global depression and the advent of the Nazi and Fascist regimes, persons began fleeing in large numbers from Germany and Italy during the early 1930s. Other groups fled from Spain, the Saar, Austria, and Czechoslovakia. By October 1933, the first convention on refugees was adopted to cope with new refugee groups created by the deepening European crisis. For the first time, an agreement guaranteed an international status for refugees. It granted them "enjoyment of civil rights" and many other specific benefits. Although the agreement was ratified by only eight states and therefore had very limited application, it proved to be a vital step toward giving refugees a defined and accepted identity under international law.

The 1933 convention was followed by other agreements intended to help specific groups of refugees: in 1935, a plan for issuing identity documents to refugees from the Saar; in 1936, a provisional agreement on the status of refugees from Germany; finally, in 1938, a full convention on the status of refugees from Germany. The latter agreement was later amended to include persons fleeing Austria. The convention, and the amendment, were nonetheless only accepted by three states.[5] Despite these agreements, many would-be refugees, especially Jews attempting to flee Germany, were turned back at European borders during the 1930s. And the whole rudimentary structure of international refugee legislation was swept away by the outbreak of the war in 1939.

Although the interwar period was characterized by uncertainty, confusion, and hesitation about refugees and their needs and rights, that period nonetheless brought forth four significant steps in the process toward acceptance and protection of refugees:

• First, an understanding that their status was legitimate, created by events beyond their control, and that refugees were entitled to some form of specific recognition as well as to the protection no longer obtainable from their state of origin;

• Second, a rudimentary, even if not always articulated, agreement on the principle of *non-refoulement* – that there should be no forced repatriation to an area where the refugee would suffer persecution;

• Third, widespread international awareness that the most urgent physical needs of the new arrivals should be met;

• Fourth, general recognition that a common or at least coordinated policy was essential to success.

The limitations of what had been achieved were, however, also clear. Recognition and acceptance of refugees were far from universal. Several of the agreements governing protection of the refugees were only accepted reluctantly and by a very limited number of countries, precisely because they broke new ground. Generosity could not be legislated or compelled but had to be genuinely felt in each asylum country. Moreover, despite some efforts, nothing could be done to persuade the governments of the countries of origin to abandon policies that were generating refugees.

Notwithstanding these limitations, the new principles represented genuine achievements. The measures taken by European states were to provide the first of several instances during the twentieth century when an outpouring of sympathy for a large group of refugees was to lead to the codification of new laws or regulations more favorable to refugees than those that had existed in the past.

The flows of refugees after World War I and between the wars were as nothing compared to the enormous flood of people sweeping across Europe after World War II. During the war itself, an estimated 27 million persons were displaced. After the war, when many displaced persons had returned to what was left of their homes, millions of refugees from Eastern Europe and from the eastern portions of Germany fled west. They were met by Western governments, by the United Nations Relief and Rehabilitation Administration (UNRRA) established by the Allies in 1943, and by about 60 voluntary agencies. Most assistance came from the United States because the countries of Western Europe had themselves suffered deeply. Nonetheless, the European countries still had to admit the refugees and grant them permission to stay until some determination on their future could be made. Their status and rights remained tenuous. They were often described as temporarily displaced persons rather than as refugees.[6]

It soon became clear, however, that most could not return to their homes safely and that they neither dared nor wished to try. In negotiations about these groups, the Soviet Union insisted on repatriation, whether voluntary or not. Although some groups were forcibly repatriated right after the war, the West increasingly came to stress that any return would have to be voluntary. In the process of the discussions and subsequent allied consultations, the West further realized that these millions of persons were not temporarily displaced but needed permanent refuge. The problem was considered so serious that more hours during the first session of the United Nations General Assembly were devoted to refugee issues than to any other subject except international security. In the course of the discussions, the General Assembly concluded that there should be no forced repatriation and that the refugee problem should be seen as "international in scope and nature."[7]

The deliberations also made clear that piecemeal efforts, like those after World War I, would prove inadequate and that the many refugee groups would have to be considered as one common problem. On July 1, 1947 the General Assembly established the International Refugee Organization (IRO), the first agency created by the new United Nations.[8] The IRO grew from a legal and social welfare agency into a worldwide network, helping refugees on an emergency basis in Europe and attempting simultaneously to arrange for them to be settled either there or on other continents. It handled protection, relief, and transport as well as initial resettlement arrangements. At its peak, it had a staff of 3,000. Its total expenditures came to more than $400 million, a considerable amount in its time.

2

Protection

The Western nations, especially the United States, welcomed the work of the IRO but did not wish to see its high level of expenditure continue. They wanted international bodies to concentrate most of their efforts on protection of refugees. As the European problem began to appear less desperate, the West looked for another structure. It found a solution in the form of two agreements, closely linked, mutually reinforcing, and intended to achieve complementary purposes.

The Statute and the Convention

The first agreement established a new office, that of the UN High Commissioner for Refugees (UNHCR), to serve as the principal agency for handling refugee problems. The statute of the office, agreed on by the General Assembly on December 14, 1950, authorized the High Commissioner to provide "international protection" for refugees and to seek "permanent solutions."

The second agreement, reached at a separate international conference in 1951, was a basic convention relating to the status of refugees. This convention absorbed under its umbrella all the refugees covered by the interwar agreements. Most important, it also provided a new definition of a refugee as a person who

> as a result of events occuring before 1 January 1951 and owing to well-founded fear of being persecuted for reasons of race, religion, nationality, membership of a particular social group or political opinion, is outside the country of his nationality and is unable or, owing to such fear, unwilling to avail himself of the protection of that country; or who, not having a nationality and being outside the country of his former habitual residence as a result of such events, is unable or, owing to such fear, is unwilling to return to it.[9]

This language set forth a global definition that in theory ensured that all groups of refugees would be treated equally by all the signatories of the document. Further, to ensure equality, the definition was followed by a listing of the rights to be accorded to refugees. These rights granted equal treatment with nationals in wide areas, including employment, property, welfare, and education, for legally admitted refugees, provided that the refugees fully conformed to the laws and regulations of their respective host countries.

The convention did, however, set some severe limits on the applicability of these generous provisions. The convention was to apply only to persons whose refugee status resulted from events that had taken place before January 1, 1951. It also permitted signatories to limit the application of the convention to events that had taken place in Europe. Most signatories, at least initially, chose to apply that geographic limitation. Thus the 1951 convention, despite its universal language, initially served mainly as an instrument for the reception and care of the trans-European refugees whose plight had directly inspired it.[10] It also failed to guarantee refugees the right of asylum, merely stating that they could not be forcibly returned to places where they would be exposed to further persecution (*non-refoulement*).

The 1951 convention represented the most significant single advance yet in refugee protection. Growing out of the work of 26 nations, it included more states than ever before in the commitment to refugees. It provided a more far-reaching definition of refugees than any earlier document and also granted them more rights. It was categorical in its injunction against forcible repatriation. It also established a direct link between itself and the High Commissioner, specifically stating that the contracting parties "undertake to co-operate with the Office of the United Nations High Commissioner . . . in the exercise of its functions, and shall in particular facilitate its duty of supervising the application of the provisions of the Convention." This provision was to become significant because the High Commissioner's mandate, while using a refugee definition virtually identical to that of the convention, set no limits regarding the time or the place of events that generated refugees. Because the General Assembly specifically reserved the right to instruct the High Commissioner to undertake activities going beyond the limits set in the convention, the High Commissioner's actions, by extension of his authority, could carry the laws and principles of refugee protection into areas in which they had not initially applied or perhaps even been expected to apply and into countries that had not signed or ratified the 1951 convention.[11]

The Protocol

The limitations embedded in the 1951 convention became increasingly onerous during the late 1950s and the 1960s. European refugee flows could usually be attributed directly or indirectly to causes that antedated 1951. But the inadequacies of the definition were painfully obvious in the face of new refugee crises in the Third World. Countries that wanted to help refugees felt constrained by the difficulty of adapting the convention to these new situations. African countries in particular felt that the convention needed to be universalized because they had to cope with numerous refugee flows that were not covered by the 1951 definition. The African states planned a conference of their own to bring international refugee principles up-to-date. They wanted especially to agree on principles and perhaps on a definition that would supersede the limitations of the 1951 definition and would help solve their own growing problems.

The High Commissioner, Felix Schnyder, shared those concerns. With the support of the Carnegie Endowment for International Peace, he arranged a meeting in Bellagio, Italy to discuss ways of arriving at a solution. On the basis of that discussion, he undertook extensive consultations with many Western governments between 1965 and 1966 to find appropriate ways to modernize the convention.[12] In 1967 the High Commissioner and his recently formed Executive Committee agreed on a protocol to the 1951 convention. That protocol removed the 1951 date from the convention and abolished the European geographic limitation, although states were free to retain the limitation if they wished (as Italy and Turkey, for example, still do).[13]

By working through the Executive Committee, the High Commissioner and interested states could reach the new agreement much more quickly than if they had gone through a lengthy negotiating procedure similar to that of 1951. They also gave the 1951 convention a more legitimate claim to universality, helping it to gain widespread acceptance by many more states than would have been interested in a document limited to Europe. This has been reflected in the number of states that have ratified either or both of the two documents. The hundredth, in March of 1986, was Papua New Guinea, a state that did not even become independent until more than 20 years after the original convention had been signed.

The Refugee Convention of the Organization
for African Unity

Refugees in Africa posed a different problem from those in Europe. Despite the steady stream of persons continuing to leave Eastern Europe, it was widely believed in 1951 that the massive flight of Europeans was for the most part finished. In Africa, however, conflicts continued and even intensified after that period. Unlike Europe, Africa was in constant upheaval. As one nation after another fought against its colonial regime or suffered from the dislocations caused by neighboring conflicts, hundreds of thousands of persons sought safety in flight.

The Africans fled essentially from three types of conflict. The first, which began in the late 1940s, were the wars of liberation. The second, which began in the 1950s, were conflicts between different nations or political groups within a single boundary, usually a boundary left by the colonial rulers. The third were the wars between neighboring countries, also often linked to artificial borders or to national or tribal animosities.

The newly independent African governments had begun to recognize as early as the 1950s that the 1951 convention did not fully meet their needs, in part because of its geographic and chronological limitations but mainly because its text did not reflect the kinds of problems facing Africa. Several times during the 1960s, member states of the Organization for African Unity (OAU), facing immense refugee problems, discussed the possibility of negotiating an African refugee agreement that would be more appropriate to the needs of the continent. Their principal objectives were to gain fair treatment for African refugees and to avoid having refugee problems become a source of political friction among African states.[14] By the late 1960s, they already found themselves with more than a million refugees on the continent and realized that they had to reach agreement urgently.[15] The 1967 protocol dealt with some of their concerns but, like the 1951 convention, did not meet all of them.

In September 1969, an assembly of 41 African heads of state and government met in Addis Ababa, Ethiopia to sign the OAU Convention Governing the Specific Aspects of Refugee Problems in Africa. That document incorporated the 1951 convention definition of a refugee but went significantly beyond that convention in important matters pertaining to protection. The African leaders added a broader definition more readily suitable to the situation that prevailed in Africa. Under that definition, the term refugee also included a person who was compelled to flee because of "external aggression, occupation, foreign domination or events seriously disturbing public order in either part or the whole of his country of origin or nationality."[16]

The OAU convention also contained the most explicit pledge by any group of governments to offer asylum and permanent settlement to refugees. It stated that

> Member States of the OAU shall use their best endeavors consistent with their respective legislations to receive refugees and to secure the settlement of those refugees who, for well-founded reasons, are unable or unwilling to return to their country of origin or nationality.

The states thus committed themselves not only to grant refugees temporary haven but even to permit them to settle permanently. This particular provision grew from the African leaders' awareness that refugees from one country might often be members of the same national or tribal groups as those of the country of asylum. It reflected a particularly generous spirit that has proven essential to the permanent settlement arrangements that have marked much of the African refugee experience.

Expansion of the High Commissioner's Mandate

Beyond the internationally agreed definitions regarding refugees, the member nations of the United Nations have expanded the mandate of the High Commissioner to categories of refugees not specifically included in the language of the original definition. Those persons, by being protected or assisted by the High Commissioner, were to become refugees or were at least to be treated as refugees by the extension of the mandate.

The original mandate was linked to the definition in the statute of the High Commissioner. The General Assembly had, however, indicated that the High Commissioner's office would be expected to discharge not only the functions enumerated in the mandate but also "such other functions as the General Assembly may from time to time confer upon it."[17] The principal instruments for expansion of the mandate have been General Assembly resolutions passed either in response to refugee crises, in approval of one or another of the High Commissioner's reports to the General Assembly, or in connection with periodic reviews undertaken when the High Commissioner's mandate, which has always been temporary, has had to be renewed.

After 1951, no occasion for special General Assembly action arose for several years, as the High Commissioner confined his activities essentially to the European refugees for which his office had been created. It did arise, however, during the flight of Chinese refugees to Hong Kong and of Algerians to Morocco and Tunisia in the 1950s. The General Assembly responded by authorizing the High Commissioner to use his "good offices" to encourage arrangements for contributions to help persons "of concern" to the international community.[18]

After that, the General Assembly frequently used the device of "good offices" resolutions to authorize the High Commissioner to play a role in refugee situations other than those in Europe.[19] It also consistently asked or authorized him over the years to assist persons "of concern." The General Assembly used some of those occasions to specify certain additional functions that the High Commissioner was to assume. It also began frequently to request that the High Commissioner support specific actions that it deemed desirable. For example, the High Commissioner was specifically authorized not only to assist Angolan refugees in the Congo during the emergency in 1961, but also to help refugees to become self-supporting and to facilitate voluntary repatriation.[20]

In 1973, the General Assembly decided to assemble and codify in one resolution the special authorities that it had granted on several earlier occasions. It asked the High Commissioner to continue his assistance and protection activities in favor of "those of concern to his office." It specified three groups: refugees within his mandate, those to whom he extended his good offices, and those he was called upon to assist by the General Assembly. It also asked him to assist in four possible solutions to various refugee problems as appropriate: voluntary repatriation, assistance in rehabilitation, integration in countries of asylum, or resettlement in other countries.[21] Through these formulations, it granted the High Commissioner the authority and responsibilty to protect and assist not only the original refugees of the mandate and the definition but also whatever other groups might be determined to need or warrant his support. It also gave him authority to undertake a wide range of actions going well beyond protection.

As other problems arose and required the High Commissioner's intervention, the General Assembly consistently expanded the range of persons included within the High Commissioner's responsibilities and functions, thus at the same time further widening the scope of the types of persons who were to be treated as if they were refugees even if the legal definition was not changed. It called for humanitarian assistance to "displaced persons" in Indochina in 1975 and the following year endorsed a resolution by the Economic and Social Council that stated that the High Commissioner's mandate extended to "refugees and displaced persons, victims of man-made disasters."[22] In 1977, to underline the importance of the High Commissioner's widened authority, the General Assembly asked all governments to support the High Commissioner in his actions, inter alia by asking them to follow humanitarian principles with respect to asylum and to observe the principle of *non-refoulement*.[23] In 1985, in response to the drought emergency in the Horn of Africa, it asked him to assist persons "in refugee-like situations" who had fled to Sudan from Chad and Ethiopia because the drought prevented them from growing food and they could not get relief supplies because of internal conflict.[24]

In response to these General Assembly resolutions, the High Commissioner's protection authority and responsibility have greatly expanded, from protection for a clearly defined and restricted group of persons to vast numbers in different if parallel situations all over the globe. The common bond between those persons may have been initially established by the different agreements created by the international community, but it was also forged by the involvement of the High Commissioner. It was the High Commissioner whose actions linked old refugees and new—those of 1951, 1967, 1969, those of his "concern," those in "refugee-like situations," and beyond. He linked them by his protection, by his actions on their behalf, and by his presence. In the process, the lines between the separate conventions and lines of authority were to become blurred, as were those between the complementary definitions. The image of the refugee as a person displaced, dispossessed, and in need was clearly etched, but the legal distinctions between different types of refugees were to become increasingly unclear, especially in developing countries where the extensions of the mandate had been most liberally applied.

The Definitions and the Concepts

Behind these various definitions, however, lay three distinct concepts and realities: behind the 1951 definition lay Western history and expectations; behind the OAU definition lay the African experience and the implications of the colonial legacy; behind the High Commissioner's mandate lay an inspired humanitarian improvisation.

The concept of "persecution" understood by the framers of the 1951 convention was based on the nature of the twentieth century totalitarian state. The authors of the definition saw Hitlerism and Stalinism. They saw the rigidly centralized structure and the omnipresent police system, as described by George Orwell, Arthur Koestler, or by others who had experienced it. In such state systems, differences of race, religion, nationality, and social or political opinion loomed large. Those states raised to the level of doctrine the concept of enemies of the state, of persons who were objectively and irretrievably hostile. Those persons and their children and their children's children would either have to be eliminated or forced out of the political process, by physical or political action. They would be the object of purposeful and pitiless pursuit. To the framers of the 1951 convention, this represented persecution, as they had seen it in the 1930s and 1940s and as they saw it extending into time.

Behind the 1951 definition of persecution, therefore, lay Western repugnance toward the kind of society that had started several wars, that had killed tens of millions of its own people as well as those of other nationalities, and that subjected its own citizens to the most far-reaching and arbitrary controls. The Western governments saw that the harshly ideological states that had assumed power in Central and Eastern Europe during the twentieth century represented danger, not protection, for certain of their citizens. The West wished to make it possible for those unprotected citizens to leave their countries if they could. Above all else, it feared that any person who had fled such a system and was forced to return would either be imprisoned or killed.[25]

The Africans had a different perception. For them, the West itself could be and had been a source of violence. It had enslaved them, seized their lands and treasures, and imposed itself upon them. They needed to fight against it to gain their own freedom. In that process, civilians might need to escape from war zones or from areas controlled by colonial powers. Those persons should be granted refuge so that they could receive protection and help. They would also need some assistance if they repatriated in case their homes had been destroyed.

The leaders of the newly independent African states could also see ahead to the problems that the continent would have after liberation. By the 1960s, when the elements of the OAU refugee convention were conceived, several African states were already at war with each other. Several were in a state of civil war. Refugees had already fled from those states. It was clear that they were not persecuted by a totalitarian system in the sense of the 1951 convention but that they nonetheless had to flee. In situations of those kinds, the government might still wish to protect but would be unable to do so.

The Africans could also see that the Western concept might have some application to their needs. Some of the newly independent African states might themselves be taken over by ideological rulers. The African leaders therefore devised a definition that would go beyond the 1951 definition while incorporating it.

Another problem for Africa was that protection and assistance would have to be offered on a mass basis, whereas the European concept had been more oriented toward individual refugee determination. The Africans perceived that in certain conflict situations persons would want to flee, and need to flee, even if they were not personally marked for persecution. Random, mindless violence, whether terrorism or war, applied against a people or against an area, might not be specifically directed at any particular person or set of persons in that area but would still kill at least some. Everyone who was there would run the risk of death or injury whether they were targets or not. Under that kind of threat, the Africans believed, large numbers of persons, as well as individuals, would be justified in fleeing and would deserve asylum. The threat was similar to that of an earthquake or a flood: not all might be killed, but all would be justified in taking flight.

The concept of refugees under the High Commissioner's mandate, unlike the European or African concept, had no fixed boundaries. It grew out of the wishes of UN governments who saw that in certain situations persons might need protection even when they did not precisely meet the language of any convention or have sought refuge in states party to the convention. The governments saw the High Commissioner as a flexible instrument that could be used to help persons in situations not specifically foreseen but still within the broad intent and spirit of refugee law and of humanitarian principles.

The UN used formulations like "persons of concern," "externally displaced persons," or "persons in refugee-like situations" to create flexibility within the general purposes of the original concepts and conventions. To them, the reality of persons who needed protection and assistance went beyond particular phrases, and they felt that the phrases could be interpreted within reason to cover many situations of genuine humanitarian need in a rapidly evolving but basically violent world. Of course, those same flexible formulations could also, if necessary, be constricted to the specific letter of the definitions contained in the conventions.

The Claim to Asylum

The principal guarantee of a refugee's safety is asylum – the refugee's ability to find a haven. The word comes from the ancient Greek term *asylon*, meaning inviolate shelter. It is the oldest and the most important element of a refugee's protection. It is part of the tradition of the Hebrew, Christian, and Muslim religions, and of Greek, Roman, and English law.[26]

It is striking and even paradoxical that, despite the expansion of international protection functions and the widening of the High Commissioner's range of activities, the basic asylum need remains that aspect of refugee needs least precisely pledged as an individual right in international law as well as that most jealously preserved as a prerogative of states. The principles at stake are basic: a state needs to control its borders and to pass judgment on those it admits; a refugee needs to find a safe haven, often quickly, and also a place to remain longer if he or she cannot safely return home. In this potential conflict of needs and interests, the states have never yielded to any international authority their own sovereign right to be the final arbiters of whom they will permit to enter.

Various types of agreements have reflected the determination of states not to surrender this element of sovereignty. During the preparatory negotiations for the Universal Declaration of Human Rights, there were some proposals that the article regarding asylum should state that "everyone has the right to seek and *to be granted* asylum," but this language was not accepted and the final version reads "to seek and *to enjoy* asylum."[27] Regional refugee accords also reflect these firm attitudes. Neither the 1954 Caracas Convention on Territorial Asylum, the 1967 Declaration of the Committee of Ministers to the Council of Europe, nor the 1969 OAU convention guaranteed a right to asylum. The OAU convention came closest with its pledge that member states of the OAU should "use their best endeavors" consistent with their respective legislations to receive refugees. The European declaration merely pledged the governments to "maintain . . . their liberal attitude." The Caracas convention reaffirmed the traditional view that "every state has the right . . . to admit into its territory such persons as it deems advisable."[28]

The search for a more generous arrangement continued for a number of years. In 1967, the UN adopted a Convention on Territorial Asylum, which did not proclaim any guaranteed right to asylum but at least reinforced the prohibition against forcible return and protected against summary rejection at the frontier.[29] Further discussion ensued, especially during the mid-1970s when refugees from Indochina were scattered across Southeast Asian waters and were frequently denied the right to land. In 1977 the UN Secretary General, in consultation with the High Commissioner, convened the Conference on Territorial Asylum, which had before it several far-reaching proposals on asylum submitted by nongovernmental working groups as well as some notes from the High Commissioner. Several proposals contained language that might have been interpreted as an obligation for states to grant asylum or to use their "best endeavors" subject to certain exceptions. But the conference was a failure, reaching no consensus even on some less sweeping asylum commitments although it made progress on some minor issues like *non-refoulement* of persons at the border and family reunion. It has never been reconvened.[30]

At the time, particularly in response to the desperate situation of the Indochinese "boat people," the Australian government proposed a formula for granting temporary asylum, but this proposal also failed to generate a consensus. Ultimately, it was not needed because the Southeast Asian states agreed to give temporary refuge while asylees awaited resettlement in the West.[31]

Thus, even after the several conventions and the expansions of the mandate, the claim of a refugee to protection still remains somewhat ambiguous. Protection resides fundamentally in the principle of *non-refoulement*, the prohibition against forcible repatriation. States that are not prepared to welcome a refugee permanently or even temporarily must at least not send that refugee back to a place where he or she might justifiably fear persecution. This right, basic to a refugee's safety, is now guaranteed by more than 100 states. The High Commissioner provides international protection in support of that right. He will recognize persons or groups as refugees and, on that basis, appeal to states to offer those refugees permanent or at least temporary asylum and not to return them against their will. He must be heard. Under the extensions of the mandate, the High Commissioner can now exercise this authority for refugees outside the strict language of the original 1951 convention and certainly well beyond that of any earlier documents.

Despite the advances in refugee law and protection represented by those provisions and practices, however, it also remains true that no individual can claim asylum as an absolute right guaranteed under international law. The grant of asylum remains the sovereign prerogative of the state to which the individual may apply, and it is a sovereign right that states can – and do – choose on occasion to withhold. There is no indication that they are more likely to surrender it now than they have been earlier. They cannot legally return a refugee forcibly to the country from which he or she fled, but they may well expel the refugee to another country or make it clear that entry is strictly temporary. The structure of refugee protection and care needs to be understood in the light of that reality, but also in the light of the High Commissioner's authority – and even responsibility – to influence the decisions of states.

3

Assistance

Although protection is their most immediate need, refugees ultimately must have more than that. They need not only a place to live but the means as well. These may in an emergency include only the most essential items, such as food, shelter, medical care, and rudimentary sanitation. They can go beyond that to include basic education, clothing, training, and counseling—even the resources to find and to establish a new home.

Since World War II, assistance for refugees has become a significant interntional expenditure. Some of the money is spent on international refugee assistance; some of it is spent after refugees arrive at their place of resettlement. It comes from different sources, moves through different channels, and is spent by different organizations in different ways. Each part of it is intended to help refugees at a different phase of their existence.

In the first years after World War II, as the ravaged countries of Western Europe received large numbers of refugees when they could not even begin to take care of the needs of their own citizens, it rapidly became clear that international assistance would be essential. This was the reason for the considerable support given to the IRO. It was also clear, however, that the contributors did not want any more funds disbursed than was necessary and preferred to have them spent for protection and for long-term solutions, not for perpetual support.[32] Of the more than $400 million that the IRO disbursed between 1947 and 1952, almost half was paid for resettlement and relocation of refugees in their countries of final destination. The portion spent on care and maintenance declined from 57 percent to 16 percent, with durable solution costs rising proportionately as refugees were settled, resettled, or, in some instances, repatriated.

After the end of the IRO period in 1952, however, more than 100,000 refugees needing further assistance still remained in camps. A special supplementary effort financed by the Ford Foundation contributed to further training to help remaining refugees settle, but the major expenditures required for durable solutions required another international effort, this one through a new arrangement termed the United Nations Refugee Fund. That fund and further aid contributed to clear the European camps during the World Refugee Year 1959–1960 totaled another $90 million for those whom High Commissioner A.R. Lindt had termed the "forgotten people" because they had languished so long in camps that their plight had ceased to arouse attention or sympathy.[33] International government expenditure to provide care and maintenance as well as resettlement support for refugees immediately after World War II thus reached a total well over $500 million. No official estimate exists on the level of private funds or of domestic government expenditures to support settlement, but these must also have been considerable.

Assistance Levels

The Western nations — especially the United States — hoped after the IRO experience that it would no longer be necessary to continue massive expenditures for assistance, and many refugee problems during the 1950s could indeed be solved with only modest infusions of funds.[34] Even those funds were not easy to come by, however. The first High Commissioner, Dr. J.G. Van Heuven Goedhart, complained in his lecture accepting the 1954 Nobel Peace Prize that he had to spend much too much time and effort raising funds.[35]

The refugee flow through Austria and Yugoslavia that followed the 1956 Hungarian uprising again brought home clearly that arrangements for asylum and protection of refugees could not in themselves solve all refugee problems. Because the Western nations did not wish to continue to make separate financing arrangements for each new group of refugees, they decided that the UNHCR needed continuing authority to administer and disburse funds for refugee assistance as well as a mechanism to oversee the proper disbursement of those funds. General Assembly Resolution 1166 of November 26, 1957 established the necessary authority and, with it, the UNHCR Executive Committee to authorize expenditures.[36] It also established an emergency fund.

The resolution nonetheless continued to reflect the Western nations' reluctance to encourage significant disbursements for refugee assistance. It stated that asylum countries should soon find the numbers of refugees reduced to the point at which they should be able to support the refugees without international assistance. It added that its own provisions were intended only to meet the "residual need" for support in certain particular situations. It specified that the emergency fund should be used only for "the most needy" groups of refugees within the High Commissioner's mandate. The language reflected the wish of the contributors to UNHCR's budget to keep assistance at modest levels and to concentrate it on durable solutions rather than on continuing maintenance of refugees in place. It was on such a basis that the international community conducted the World Refugee Year and made a special effort to engage in the clearing and closing of camps so that no refugees remained unsettled.

For a decade and a half after that, many refugee crises

could be adequately met by small-scale or at least temporary arrangements. Although such crises followed one another with depressing regularity, particularly in Africa, most were solved without provisions for sizeable long-term assistance funds. Until the mid-1970s, the UNHCR's annual assistance program generally remained at modest levels. In 1971 and 1972, for example, the programs were at the $7 and $8 million level respectively. These funds went mainly to assist refugees in several African countries, particularly the former Belgian Congo, though some funds also went to Europe and Asia.[37]

Expenditures for refugee assistance exploded in the mid-1970s with the collapse of the Republic of Vietnam and of the Lon Nol government in Cambodia. The exodus from Indochina accelerated in 1978 and 1979 with the boat people. It was to be supplemented in the following years by large new arrivals of refugees fleeing Afghanistan to Pakistan and others fleeing from various parts of Ethiopia into Somalia and the Sudan. The levels of UNHCR assistance rose rapidly, to $90 million by 1976, more than $100 million by 1977, then to $280 million by 1979.

Since 1980, UNHCR's assistance requirements have been at a consistently high level, despite some variations from year to year. During 1980, requirements went over the half-billion dollar mark, reaching $510 million. They declined slightly in 1981, to $487 million, and then continued down to $420 and $405 million the following years. Between 1984 and 1986 they rose again in response to a new African refugee crisis, and they remained between $450 and $460 million during those years.

Under those generally constant assistance levels, however, there has been some shift in the geographical distribution pattern. From 1982 to 1987, the proportion of assistance for Southeast Asian refugees has declined somewhat (from 28 to 21 percent of the program) as more persons have been resettled. The portion for aid to Afghans has remained generally constant, between 22 and 24 percent, but the percentages for two areas have risen: Africa, from 32 to 38 percent, and the Americas, from 9 to 15 percent. There has also been a shift in funding toward durable solutions and away from maintenance, as the emergency flows of the late 1970s and early 1980s have been absorbed into more regular programs of resettlement and local installation. Between 1982 and 1987, the portion of the High Commissioner's program devoted to care and maintenance, such as expenditure for food and medical care, declined from 67 to 55 percent, while the amount dedicated to durable solutions, such as resettlement or permanent installation, rose from 29 to 40 percent. Nonetheless, this remains a far cry from the 1960s and early 1970s, when well over half the UNHCR's budget was normally spent for funding durable solutions, or from earlier times when more than 80 percent was devoted to that purpose.

The Extended Mandate in Assistance

Just as the mandate of the High Commissioner has at various times been expanded to give him and the office greater protection functions, it has also been expanded to authorize additional types of assistance. Moreover, the UNHCR has on a number of occasions been specificallly asked by the General Assembly to assume special assistance responsibilities with respect to one or another group of refugees. As part of the preparation for refugee repatriation to Zimbabwe in 1979 and 1980, for example, the 1979 UNHCR resolution of the General Assembly asked the UNHCR, inter alia, not only "to promote durable and speedy solutions through voluntary repatriation or return," but also to provide "subsequent assistance in rehabilitation."[38] When refugees from Djibouti began repatriating to Ethiopia between 1982 and 1984 and needed help in resuming their former lives, the General Assembly asked the High Commissioner "to continue his efforts to mobilize humanitarian assistance for the relief and rehabilitation of certified voluntary returnees" to Ethiopia.[39] The General Assembly made a similar request in 1984 regarding returnees to Chad.[40] The High Commissioner is now expected to provide assistance not only to refugees but also to voluntary returnees when necessary for their reintegration into developing countries. Such repatriation programs are not funded out of the UNHCR's regular budget but are special programs funded separately by interested donors. This has usually meant that some repatriation programs are adequately funded whereas others are not. Such nonrepatriation programs as the special assistance offered in 1984–1985 to refugees fleeing from drought-stricken portions of Ethiopia and Chad into Sudan, however, will usually be added to the regular budget after a year or two, even if they began as special programs.[41]

The General Assembly has begun in recent years to invite the High Commissioner to participate in development assistance to promote durable solutions. This request came in two stages. First, in its 1985 resolution regarding the Second International Conference on Assistance to Refugees in Africa, the General Assembly emphasized "the vital importance of the complementarity of refugee aid and development assistance."[42] At that point it stressed the primary role of the United Nations Development Program (UNDP) by requesting the UNDP to "increase its effort to mobilize additional resources for refugee-related development projects and, in general, to promote and co-ordinate with the host countries and the donor community the integration of refugee-related activities into national development planning."

Later, the General Assembly asked the High Commissioner to go further. It expressed its appreciation for the work done by the High Commissioner "to put into practice the concept of development-oriented assistance to refugees and returnees," as had been requested at the conference, and urged him "to continue that process, wherever appropriate, in full cooperation with appropriate international agencies, and, further, urged governments to support these efforts."[43] The General Assembly reiterated its request that the UNDP "increase its efforts to mobilize additional resources for refugee-related development projects," showing that the General Assembly still wanted development agencies to play the primary role in advancing the financing and execution of such projects, but allowing a greater role than in the past for the UNHCR.[44] This means that the UNHCR, beginning as an agency that provided help for durable solutions for refugees, must now often maintain long-term relief programs, provide for the rehabilitation of returnees, and also play a role in promoting and coordinating development aid.

Forms of Assistance

As the UNHCR mandate for assistance has expanded, the types of assistance offered to refugees have evolved along with the number of people and the types of situations for which assistance is administered. These developments reflect the greater length of time that refugees have had to spend in camps, the fact that most of the world's refugees are now rural and do not have access to city services, and the growing proportion of refugees in Third World countries where many services often have to be internationally provided because the asylum country is too poor to offer them. When many refugees and their families have to remain in camps for a number of years in an area with virtually no infrastructure and few resources, assistance can and does reach significant levels on a total even if not on per capita basis.

Assistance must include such items as food, longer-term shelter, clothing, household utensils, health and sanitation facilities, trained personnel, water distribution, education and perhaps vocational training, social services and counseling—especially in long-lasting refugee situations in which the psychological impact can become particularly onerous—as well as administration.[45] Each of these items in turn contains a host of subsidiary items.[46] Administering such assistance is not unlike running a small town or even a small city. In camps containing tens of thousands of refugees, as in Pakistan, Somalia, or Sudan, the provision of relief supplies can be a significant management task involving large numbers of staff and usually requiring some expert experience in administration and budget management as well. Much of the actual work on these assistance items is carried on by specialized agencies or personnel, but the funds are usually channeled through the UNHCR.

Durable Solutions

From the standpoint of the international community and the UNHCR, refugee assistance cannot be an end in itself. The High Commissioner's assigned task has always been to provide solutions to refugee problems, not just to keep the refugees in place. The forms those solutions can take have long been prescribed: repatriation to the country of origin, settlement in the asylum country, or resettlement in yet another country. Sometimes, when none of the three solutions can be reached, a makeshift solution is to arrange programs that permit refugees to earn some modest income for self-sufficiency or to practice new as well as traditional skills. This has the advantage of keeping refugees actively engaged in useful activity, It is not a lasting solution but leaves all those options open.

Repatriation

This is the classic ideal solution because it returns refugees to their homeland, to familiar surroundings, to their friends and family – able to resume normal lives. It was not a solution in the 1940s and 1950s, when few refugees were willing to return to the Soviet Union or Eastern Europe (although some were at first sent back), but it could be used extensively in Africa as colonial wars ended and exiled populations could return to the newly independent states. It is still used in Africa. It is also frequently possible in Latin America, where many refugees repatriate when regimes or their policies change. In 1986, for example, an estimated 240,000 refugees were able to return home, mainly in Africa but about 27,000 in Latin America as well.[47]

Unfortunately, it is a solution that has been difficult to apply to many refugee groups during the 1980s, because conditions in many countries of origin have not changed sufficiently to permit all refugees to return.[48] An example is the repatriation of thousands of refugees to El Salvador from Honduras. Many have returned informally, without participating in any established program, as they tired of camp conditions and as the situation in the areas around their immediate homes may have improved sufficiently to permit and even encourage return. Others returned in a more structured way, flying to San Salvador in an aircraft chartered by the Intergovernmental Committee for Migration (ICM). The ICM has also attempted to monitor what has happened to them to make certain that they were safe after their return. It reports that no particular harm has befallen the returnees, but the ICM is not in a position to observe what may happen to all repatriates all the time. On the other hand, a study by the American Civil Liberties Union asserts that a number have been abducted, murdered, beaten, and arrested.[49]

Another controversial program, between 1982 and 1984, was the repatriation of refugees from Djibouti to Ethiopia. Many of them repatriated spontaneously and others as part of a UNHCR program that cost several million dollars to complete.[50] About 32,000 were estimated to have returned, about one-third of them in an organized manner, but at least 10,000 are reported to have remained in Djibouti despite considerable encouragement on the part of the Djibouti authorities for them to leave. There were persistent international press rumors that the refugees repatriated unwillingly under pressure from the UNHCR and Ethiopia and that they suffered harm upon their return.[51] As one scholar indicated, those who had fled from violence might well be prepared to repatriate once the violence had ceased or had eased, but those who had fled for political reasons would not wish to repatriate until there had been changes in the basic political situation from which they fled.[52]

Repatriation may thus pose special legal, assistance, and humanitarian problems. Refugees are often uncertain about going home, especially when they are not certain what will happen to them and their families. Few want to be among the first. It is often necessary – as was done in El Salvador and in Ethiopia – for some to go in advance and report directly to others on what they found. It is also often an expensive program because the homes and the lands of the refugees may either have deteriorated or been taken by others. Frequently refugees take nothing when they flee, and they need a great deal of help to get started again when they repariate. On the other hand, their adjustment is often easier than that of refugees who do not return to their homeland.

There is a distinction to be made between refugees who "repatriate" and those who "return." The former are those who go home after a lengthy stay abroad during which they were recognized and assisted as refugees. The latter are those who may not have even formally sought asylum or who, if they did seek it, were rejected and who either chose to go back or were sent back. Persons returning can usually fit back into their previous environment with less difficulty than those who were refugees and are formally repatriated, especially if the returnees did not remain outside their country of origin for long.

Settlement in Place

Settlement in the country of first asylum has been an appropriate durable solution for certain groups of refugees. Refugees from Pakistan and India exchanged countries upon partition. Many refugees from Eastern Europe have settled in Germany or Austria, just as many refugees from Latin America have settled in Spain and many Spaniards in Latin America. When the countries of asylum are contiguous to the countries of origin, or when the cultures are similar or complementary, settlement in place often offers an ideal solution.

Settlement has most often been possible in Africa, many times in connection with moves to an aslyum country in which the population had some feeling of kinship for the refugees, as in the case of Rwanda and Burundi. It has also often been used in cases where no immediate kinship may have existed but where refugees are welcomed as people in genuine need. There have been altogether well over 100 settlements established in Africa over the years. Some are small. Others, like Katumba or Mishamo in Tanzania, have a population of tens of thousands of refugees. Mishamo alone is almost as large as the state of Rhode Island.[53]

The exact cost of the settlement policy in Africa cannot be calculated. Settlements have represented as much as one-half of the UNHCR's budget for Africa during a number of years, except for major emergencies such as during 1980 or 1985. Many of these settlements have taken several years to finish. They have usually been constructed under the general supervision of the UNHCR with one or another major voluntary agency acting as principal coordinator and contractor. Any settlement takes considerable planning, not only for infrastructure and housing arrangements but also for coordination with the local populations and economy.

Basic to any settlement is available land, which is provided by the national government free of charge. It is often not the highest quality land, but must be good enough to permit sustained agricultural production after some improvements, such as water or access roads. Another important element is a stable and secure environment. A number of settlement projects in Uganda and in southern Sudan have had to be abandoned for security reasons. It is vital that the new refugee community be accepted by neighboring communities. Special arrangements are often made to invite children from those communities to use the settlement's primary schools, or for families to use the clinics, so that the neighbors can see some advantages for themselves in the settlement.

Not all settlements succeed. Some fail because of security reasons. A number do not succeed because they did not fit into national development plans or because they were left with a top heavy infrastructure that could not be sustained by the income from the settlement itself. In some instances the refugees retire from market production and return to subsistence agriculture because they do not believe that they are getting fair prices for their goods. In other cases, the sites that have been selected prove not to be as productive as had been expected, or the transportation costs are higher than originally planned.

These problems should not obscure the central achievement of the settlements, although they show that settlements need to be monitored and perhaps helped longer than had been anticipated. The settlements have provided new homes and offered new opportunities to hundreds of thousands of refugees and have permitted them and their families to return to normal and productive lives in environments sufficiently familiar to encourage a relatively good adjustment. Most of all, they have constituted an extraordinary example of national generosity on the part of the African governments and communities that have made the land and the facilities available.

Resettlement

Resettlement, involving a move by refugees to a country other than the country of first asylum, has often been decried for a number of good reasons. It usually involves taking refugees far from their original homes and cultures into different climates, different modes of life, and different value systems. It can be the most wrenching of all the solutions. Nonetheless, many refugees have opted for resettlement because it often brings them into thriving communities and economies. Some countries are concerned that resettlement may actually encourage people to become refugees.

There can be no question about the extent and the importance of resettlement as a solution. From 1975 through 1986, a total of almost 2 million refugees have resettled, more than half of them from Indochina. More than a million have come to the United States, 150,000 to Canada and France, and almost 150,000 to Australia.[54] The operation has been highly expensive for resettlement countries. For example, the U.S. Coordinator for Refugee Affairs has estimated that in Fiscal Year 1987 the United States will spend a total of $638 million on resettlement, the funds being divided between the budgets of the Department of State ($109 million), the Department of Health and Human Services ($414 million), and the Department of Agriculture ($115 million). These expenditures include overseas costs, such as language training and transportation, as well as domestic costs after arrival, such as health care, food stamps, welfare, and some reimbursed state programs.[55] The costs for other resettlement countries are not as high but are certainly significant as well, suggesting that in any given year overall refugee resettlement costs may be well over $1 billion and perhaps close to $2 billion. This figure is certainly below the peak of the early 1980s, but it is still a considerable sum.

Resettlement as a solution has been more intensively studied than any other, in part because it is on our doorstep but also because it represents a genuine opportunity to see how a large group of persons who have undergone a traumatic change in their lives can adjust to a new environment.[56] It is also a test of the capacity of both developed societies and incoming refugees to adapt to each other, especially as more and more refugees come to the West from the Third World and not from Eastern Europe.

The conclusions of these studies not surprisingly suggest that the capacity of resettled refugees to adjust de-

pends on many factors. Age is important; the young generally adapt much faster than the old. Earlier associations
and knowledge are important; those who speak the host
language and who have had earlier contact with the host
nationality adjust better. Nationality and culture are important; some nationalities and cultures, like the Vietnamese or the East European, adjust faster than the Laotian or
the Afghan. Persons who were in the middle class or in the
professions generally adjust better than others, especially
once they can find positions corresponding to their earlier
activities. The receiving community is also important; a
large and embracing community (such as the Vietnamese
communities in Paris, Sydney, and Orange County in California, or the Cuban community in Miami) can usually help
refugees get a better start than if they are on their own or in
a small community. The culture of the receiving country is
also a factor. Most refugees prefer to resettle in a relatively
heterogenous society like the United States rather than in a
homogeneous society like Japan.

Another question of growing concern has been the welfare expenditure required to maintain refugees, sometimes
for years after their arrival. In the United States, this is
reflected in the national and the state budgets. When some
refugees, particularly young ones engaged in study programs, remain on welfare for extended periods, they may
fall into a dependency pattern that will become increasingly
difficult to break and that can generate a popular reaction
against the arrival of new refugees.

The refugees who adjust best are the children. Educa-
tors in California speak admiringly of what Vietnamese
children have brought to the educational system by their
determination to learn and to succeed. It is by now clear
that many of those children will make major contributions
to their chosen fields and will represent a genuine gain for
their countries of resettlement. For the parents of those
children, the success of the younger generation is often
compensation for all of their hardships. Refugees often flee
not primarily to make a new life for themselves but to give

their children a chance to grow up in a free and open environment. Even for children, however, conclusions as to adjustment cannot yet be reached. Adjustment occurs in several phases. Only the first few phases have so far been observed for such groups or the Indochinese. At least a decade will have to pass before any definitive conclusions can be reached.[57] Earlier groups from Europe have integrated well, but the cultural and ethnic differences between more recent groups and the populations of their country of resettlement are greater than in the past.

When cultural and professional gaps are large, when the refugee community is small, and when the society is homogeneous and not accustomed to strangers, resettlement may indeed not be a desirable option for refugees. When the reverse conditions exist, it can work well. Under the best conditions, it will ultimately be a gain for the resettlement country.

Refugees and Development

As more and more refugees have fled into developing rather than developed countries, questions have been raised about how best to take account of the refugee presence in Third World development plans and how to help refugees fit into those plans.

The High Commissioner began to convene special discussions on this subject in 1983.[58] There have also been studies and discussions separate from the meetings.[59] The UNHCR Executive Committee has discussed the matter every year since 1983, and many delegates from developed and developing countries have supported the principle that refugee assistance should be better coordinated with general development assistance. The essential principle that is beyond dispute is that successful integration of refugees into a new society requires not only assistance for refugees but also coordination of refugee and development aid, as well as some infrastructural improvements. Linked with this are such proposals as an early removal from dependency, the early initiation of self-help projects, and coordinated help for the refugees and the local population.

At the 1986 Executive Committee session, the UNHCR indicated several further approaches. One of them would be to have special development aid for "refugee-affected countries," providing preferential treatment and supplementary assistance for countries that harbor large quantities of refugees. The UNHCR has also moved to involve development agencies earlier in refugee relief projects to provide more effective coordination between refugee and development projects.[60]

Although a general consensus on the principles for coordinating refugee aid and development plans has existed for several years, actual implementation has been slow. Coordination between the UNHCR and many development agencies has been difficult to arrange because they plan in different time frames. The UNHCR needs to implement programs rapidly to take care of the refugees. Development agencies tend to act much more deliberately because development is considered a long-term operation and projects must be examined at length before they are approved and implemented. The UNHCR and the refugees may have an interest in having refugee assistance included in development programs or at least coordinated with them, but the development agencies and the asylum countries may not have a similar incentive. Many countries even worry that aid for refugees might be taken from aid for their nationals, or that it might go into refugee areas and be lost when and if the refugees move. Those countries have increasingly called for the implementation of "additionality," under which refugee aid or aid derived from a refugee presence should be supplementary to the assistance levels that the country would receive if it harbored no refugees.

Countries that fund refugee programs would be prepared to finance well-conceived projects that link refugee and development plans or programs. Voluntary agencies remain interested and have implemented a number of smaller projects, including fisheries and some small-scale farming and production. But to move from concepts to programs, from broad terms to actual implementation, and from informal discussion to actual coordination by the agencies concerned has always been difficult. Until those problems are solved, refugee and development aid will not be fully coordinated. Nonetheless, such coordination remains an important concern because it can help overcome growing popular and political resistance in Third World countries to the reception of large numbers of refugees and also because it can maximize the well-being of refugees and the surrounding communities.

4

The Organizations and
the Structure

A large number of organizations has emerged over the past four decades to minister to refugee needs as the size and complexity of the refugee problem have expanded. Some of these organizations are intergovernmental; others are nongovernmental or charitable. Some organizations with primary responsibilities outside the refugee area have also become involved, creating a considerable network. Different organizations play different but complementary roles, as do different governments.

The UN High Commissioner for Refugees

The High Commissioner stands at the center of the structure of refugee protection and care. He is both a person and an agency, being designated by the United Nations as a specific person but also having a considerable staff. Dr. van Heuven Goedhart recalled that, when he first inspected his domain in January 1951, it consisted of three empty rooms and a secretary.[61] Now it occupies the wings of two large Geneva office buildings, has 80 delegates in offices around the world, and employs more than 1,500 regular staff personnel as well as hundreds on a temporary basis.

The High Commissioner is both the conscience and the agent of the world community. As the conscience, he must remind nations of the basic commitment that they made to receive refugees and to treat them according to agreed-upon standards. As the agent, he must disburse large sums of assistance funds and manage a sizeable organization efficiently and effectively.

As discussed in earlier chapters, the High Commissioner's functions and his mandate have grown over the years.[62] In a changing world, with new types of crises arising everywhere, he has been asked to provide protection and/or assistance to ever larger and more diverse groups.[63]

The UNHCR has also expanded in geographic terms. After being concentrated in Europe in the early 1950s, it became involved in the African refugee problem with the Algerians in Morocco and Tunisia. Under the "good offices" concept, it expanded slowly into a global operation. Under High Commissioner Poul Hartling, the office assumed vast new functions in virtually every part of the world.[64] The High Commissioners did not seek their new responsibilities; the changing international situation imposed those responsibilities.

The expansion of the High Commissioner's functions has required a delicately adjusted balance of the many interests that are reflected on the UNHCR's Executive Committee. That committee consisted largely of Western countries when it was first established. The first African member, Tunisia, joined in 1958. More African and other Third World countries followed in subsequent expansions of the committee. The largest single group on the 41-member committee is still the European, with 15 members, but Africa is now represented by 11 countries. Several major asylum countries, such as Pakistan or Somalia, are not full members of the committee but attend its formal meetings as observers. Since 1980 the chairmanship of the committee customarily alternates between representatives of countries that provide the funds – the developed world – and those that now offer asylum to the largest number – the developing world.

The Intergovernmental Committee for Migration

The ICM was established at the end of 1951. Like other organizations then being created, it was intended to take up some of the functions that had been carried out by the IRO. Because its operations were to be concentrated largely on those who had remained in Europe after the war, it was first called the Intergovernmental Committee for European Migration (ICEM).[65] Its primary tasks were to make arrangements for the transport of migrants and refugees and, in particular, to increase the volume of migration from Europe.

Like the UNHCR, the ICM found that its role did not cease with the postwar movement of refugees. It was called upon to help when refugees fled from Hungary after the 1956 uprising. It moved 150,000 persons in six months. Later, it moved another 18,000 after the 1968 repression of the Prague Spring in Czechoslovakia. Its most massive tasks, however, arose after 1975, when hundreds of thousands of refugees began to flee Indochina. The ICM arranged transport for most of those refugees, especially to the United States but also to other countries. It has also consistently played a role in the movement of Latin American refugees, either in their flight or in their repatriation. The Latin American interest in the ICM has been reflected in the prominent membership of Latin American countries on its governing board.

The ICM has a central role in the travel of individual refugees who may need to be moved very quickly out of a country of first asylum as part of their protection arrangements. The ICM can often handle such travel more effectively than a commercial travel office because it usually knows what special routing and clearances might be necessary. In such operations, as in many others, the ICM complements the UNHCR. About two-thirds of ICM operations, amounting in recent years to about $70 million of its total budget, are dedicated to refugee operations, although in the peak years of the Indochinese resettlement its refugee budget rose to well over $100 million.

In the spring of 1987, the ICM constitution was revised to expand the organization's mandate for assisting in the growing domain of international migration. Many of the new provisions represent codification of authority that had already been granted on a provisional basis to deal with ongoing problems as they arose, but the totality of the provision makes it clear that the ICM can play a more considerable role than in the past if the international community wishes it to do so. Once the new constitution is approved, the organization will be called the International Organization for Migration.

Other Intergovernmental Organizations

A number of other UN organizations play a role in helping refugees. The single most important, particularly in emergency assistance and in relief operations, is the World Food Program (WFP), which for the past decade has provided most of the food to meet refugee needs.[66] In 1985, for example, two-thirds of all refugee food was supplied by the WFP.[67] That assistance has been valued at about $100 million or more virtually every year of the 1980s. The WFP has been particularly important because it has often been able to draw food rapidly from its stocks to meet emergencies. Its officials have also joined with the UNHCR officers in many visits to asylum countries to assess refugee food needs and make arrangements to meet them.

The United Nations Volunteers (UNV) have played a helpful role. The volunteers have worked in refugee programs on several continents and in many countries. They often appear at some of the most difficult refugee sites. In 1985, UNVs were working in Djibouti, Honduras, Malaysia, Somalia, and Sudan. Most of the UNVs come from Third World countries.

The UNDP helps administer refugee programs in countries in which the UNHCR is not itself represented. The UNDP has also been moving toward a larger role in the coordination between refugee aid and development assistance. This collaboration has not always functioned smoothly because the UNHCR has to function on an annual program basis, even in administering long-term solutions, whereas the UNDP must operate on the basis of long-term programs. The UNDP also has a principal commitment to nationals rather than to refugee populations. Although these divergences in priorities and operational calendars have sometimes inhibited or complicated collaboration, efforts on both sides have led to some effective cooperation. Both organizations are now committed to expanding it, especially by bringing the UNDP into refugee operations in developing countries at an earlier stage.

Other organizations are also involved. The International Labor Organization (ILO) has collaborated with the UNHCR in more countries than any other UN organization, principally on projects to help promote refugee self-sufficiency and income. The United Nations Children's Fund (UNICEF) has worked with the UNHCR in a number of areas, including water exploration and development. The International Committee of the Red Cross and the League of Red Cross and Red Crescent Societies also play roles in refugee programs. Other intergovernmental organizations have also worked under the coordination of the High Commissioner.[68]

The Voluntary Agencies

The voluntary agencies are the main operational arms and legs of the refugee care and support structure. Long before governments began funding refugee programs on a consistently large scale, asylum-seekers were finding help in churches, homes, and aid centers organized and financed by private funds and organizations. Because the UNHCR has not been operational, it has often called on voluntary organizations to carry out the actual work with refugees in the field.

Nongovernmental organizations provide many of the people who actually conduct an operation, run a hospital, direct a school, organize a camp, arrange the digging of a well or the building of a road, or simply help out in an emergency situation. Some agencies are staffed by expatriates, some by nationals of the asylum country, some by refugees themselves, and most by a mixture of all these groups. In some instances, an official government agency will conduct or coordinate a general operation, with voluntary organizations cooperating with that agency.

There are so many agencies working with refugees that it is impossible to generalize about them. There are hundreds in the United States alone and thousands all over the world. Some, like the large German and Japanese agencies, obtain significant government and other contributions on a regular basis. Others depend on voluntary funds and on special contracts for particular programs. Some operate across the globe – Care, Church World Service, Oxfam, Médecins Sans Frontières, the International Rescue Committee, or World Vision, for example. Others, such as Africare, concentrate on one continent or area. Some, like Lutheran World Relief or Catholic Relief Services, are denominational. Others, like Save the Children Fund, are not. Some, like Euro-Action Accord, a consortium of agencies, concentrate on development-related projects. Others, like the International Catholic Migration Commission, concentrate on resettlement. Still others, like the Tanganyikan Christian Relief Society, concentrate on settlements for the integration of refugees into countries of first asylum. Others concentrate on emergency or post-emergency relief work. Most agencies come from the industrialized nations but many, like Sudan Aid or the Malaysian Red Crescent, originate in countries of asylum and play a key role in the appropriate asylum country.[69]

One reason why the UNHCR has not itself needed to conduct operations in the field is that the use of voluntary agencies offers a number of real advantages. The agencies can usually bring experienced people into an emergency quickly. They can provide a wide variety of expertise that could not be attained in an international bureaucracy without keeping a large staff permanently on hand. Their experience and competence can be valuable in new situations in which local agencies and governments do not know how to handle an emergency. They offer great flexibility because some agencies or mix of agencies can provide trained and sometimes hard-to-find specialists.

Beyond operational advantages, however, lie other factors that are vital to a successful refugee operation. Voluntary agencies often generate understanding and sympathy for the operations in which they are engaged and for refugee care in general. They offer, in the dedicated personalities of their volunteers, a human element for which there is no substitute. Many of their staff are prepared to work long hours under grueling conditions in emergency situations. The 1987 kidnaping of some medical staff of Médecins San Frontières in Somalia underlines the hazards and sacrifices that agency personnel may face. They also provide a caring human atmosphere essential in dealing with refugees whose lives may have been completely shattered. This has been important in all types of refugee situations, but especially in emergencies, when refugees need great care and attention to overcome the trauma of flight, and in resettlement. Many refugees need such dedicated support not only for the first days but often for weeks after their arrival in a new country. It is impossible to overstate the enormous importance of the role that volunteers, many of them from church or community families, play when refugees and their children first arrive and have to start a new life.

Although some of the voluntary agencies receive administrative funds from the UNHCR, many contribute not only personnel but funds to assist in operations. The amount that they contribute is not calculable because agencies operate on different budget structures and arrangements, but it can be estimated at about $20 million a year for the work that they do with the UNHCR and probably more than that when worldwide expenditures are considered.

The Governments

Different countries play different roles. A basic role falls to the donor countries that contribute funds for refugee programs. These are generally the governments of the industrialized states. The United States is the largest contributor overall, the European Community usually second, and Japan third. After them, Germany, the United Kingdom, Canada, Sweden, Italy, Norway, and Denmark each contributed more than $20 million in 1986 in support of global refugee programs.[70] Many of these countries, especially in North America, Europe, and Oceania, also resettle large numbers of refugees every year. These countries thus provide not only the funds but another vital element in the functioning of the system.

The asylum countries, in which refugees receive their first asylum and often settle, are for the most part in Africa, in Latin America, and in the long southern rim along the Eurasian mainland, from Turkey to Hong Kong. The countries of first asylum bear the immediate brunt of the refugee arrivals. They have the sometimes difficult task of persuading their own population to provide shelter and haven as well as to share some of their own resources. They have to suffer the political and possibly military consequences if the countries of origin believe that refugees are engaged in hostile activities. Botswana, Pakistan, Thailand, and Zambia are among those that have been subjected to military attacks in 1987 and, in some instances, earlier. They may also be called upon ultimately to integrate the refugees on their own land. In a very real sense, therefore, the asylum countries are also donor countries, accepting the domestic and international political consequences of shielding refugees and also providing land, often by the thousands and tens of thousands of acres, to enable the refugees to remain and settle.

The resources dedicated to refugee protection, relief, and long-term solutions are immense. The half-billion dollar budget of the UNHCR is only one element. Other international agencies also have large budgets. Each country of asylum and resettlement bears a number of costs itself. Some of the costs, like the administrative costs of maintaining a government bureaucracy, may be hidden in other budgets; others, like payments to resettled refugees, may be easier to calculate. But it is probably no exaggeration to state that total global expenditures may amount to $5 billion or more every year. These are significant funds at a time of shrinking budgets in every industrialized society, and their availability on a continuing basis over the last 10 years has reflected a genuine and generous commitment.

The Structure

These many governments, international organizations, private agencies, and others collaborate in a global structure designed to take care of refugee needs in emergencies and beyond. They are expected to move quickly to help receive refugees virtually anywhere in the world. They can also save an individual refugee who may have escaped and who needs to move on urgently and discreetly. They can establish a settlement or a travel plan for tens of thousands or arrange a medical evacuation for a single individual.

The structure functions with considerable flexibility and generosity. It works with a combination of support, sacrifice, and mutual tolerance. As with every human endeavor, there is always the political temptation. Some nations play favorites with refugees. Some prefer certain types of solutions over others. Some become apprehensive when they are pressured to change the traditional roles they have worked out and accepted. But for an enterprise of such scope and complexity, the collaboration is remarkably successful. Arguments that may arise in the Executive Committee or in the field are toned down and carefully contained to avoid disrupting the consensus that lies at the foundation of the structure and that usually represents the best interests of the refugees.

What must now be considered is whether that same structure can deal with the tasks of the future. As the next chapters will illustrate, the fact that that so many refugees have been in place for so long poses new dilemmas, as does the direct arrival in industrialized countries of asylum seekers from distant Third World trouble spots.[71] It remains to be seen whether a structure that was designed 40 years ago and that has evolved to cope with certain types of problems can also deal with these new and urgent issues.

5

The Traditional Refugees

There are now refugees virtually everywhere in the world, on every continent and in almost all countries. Sometimes they are starkly evident, in special camps and in areas that may have been only minimally populated until they arrived. At other times they are inconspicuous, mingling with the population and unknown even to local authorities and to organizations that might wish to help them. Sometimes they show themselves because they need and want help; sometimes they do not because they are afraid of being expelled. There is no way of knowing exactly how many refugees there may be at any given moment. But any census carried out since 1980 or 1981 has usually arrived at a total of somewhere between 10 and 12 million.

Since about 1980, the world refugee population has remained stable with several groups growing, others have declined. Assistance funds have been harder to find as other urgent global needs have appeared, and some new ideas for refugee aid have foundered in part because of resource difficulties. Refugee law has evolved somewhat to cope with the new situation, but is now also under pressure for retrenchment. Many refugees are still living in a state of grave uncertainty, in provisional arrangements such as camps, hostels, or other quarters that might have been put at their disposal only temporarily. From the visible emergency of flight, they have passed to the invisible emergency of stagnation.

The global refugee population consists of several major groups, many of which first sought refuge between 7 and 10 years ago and have been living in temporary status ever since that time. The largest flows are Indochinese, African, Afghans, and various nationalities in the Americas.[72] Smaller groups can be found elsewhere. Several new groups, such as Iranians and Sri Lankans, create special problems because of their wide-ranging travel. They are considered separately in the next chapter.

Indochinese

Indochinese refugees, particularly the Vietnamese, have stamped their image and their cause indelibly on the conscience of the world. The boat people, haggard, emaciated, desperate, bobbing in frail and overcrowded craft on the choppy waters of the Gulf of Thailand, proved all too easy a prey to pirates on the water and to rejection when they tried to land. They often fell victim to the random cruelties of the sea or to the more calculated cruelties of their fellowmen. But they also aroused great sympathy and support, more perhaps than any group of refugees since the Hungarians in 1956, and that sympathy helped provide a welcome for other refugees that were to follow them in succeeding years. They inaugurated what might be termed the current phase of refugee care.[73]

The Vietnamese

The boat people were not the first modern refugees in or from Indochina. Those were the almost 1 million, mainly Catholics, who fled south to the Republic of Vietnam after the division of Vietnam in 1954. Later, during the second

Indochina war, many members of the middle class left Vietnam. They fled in small numbers, often in family groups, and did not always formally register as refugees. They settled in France, other European countries, or the United States to wait out events. That flow accelerated after the 1973 Paris accords were signed and as the cease-fire failed to hold.

After the fall of Saigon and of South Vietnam in 1975, the trickle of refugees became a flood. An estimated 200,000 persons left Indochina within weeks. A good 150,000 of those fled from Vietnam. They included many who had fought with the Americans, more of the middle class, and others who were terrified at the prospect of a Communist state. They fled on commercial or U.S. military flights, passing through a Saigon airport processing center named "Dodge City," or by small boats from many places on the Vietnamese coast to U.S. naval and charter vessels waiting in international waters. Most came to the United States, where they were met with warmth and offers of resettlement. By the end of the year, all emergency processing centers in the United States had been closed and the refugees were for the most part established in their new homes.

Vietnamese in smaller numbers continued leaving even after 1975, mainly for Europe or for the United States. They left Vietnam over water to several Southeast Asian countries or over land across Cambodia to Thailand. Many were professional persons, but a certain number were fishermen who either brought out a group of people or their own family members.

Three years after the fall of Saigon, the Socialist Republic of Vietnam introduced several measures to accelerate socialization of the Vietnamese economy and society. These steps deepened the mood of despair of many middle class Vietnamese, especially of Chinese origin. They also contributed to a bitter confrontation with the People's Republic of China, already disturbed by extensive Vietnamese involvement in Cambodia. After the Vietnamese government indicated that Vietnamese of Chinese origin were free to go to China, more than 150,000 fled there by the end of 1978. Other Vietnamese by the tens of thousands took to boats with the apparent encouragement, or at least acquiescence, of the government. The flow increased month by month, culminating in departures of more than 50,000 during both May and June of 1979. Although several Southeast Asian countries initially refused landing to many of the boat people, forcing the boats off even if it meant that the passengers drowned, more than 375,000 Vietnamese were living in makeshift camps across Southeast Asia by July of 1979 when an international conference was hurriedly convened to deal with their plight. The world had initially underestimated the gravity of the problem, but the dimensions of the boat exodus aroused intense international concern.

The conference, held in Geneva, led to an understanding involving a number of commitments by different parties that were affected by the outpouring of refugees. Vietnam agreed to cease encouraging the outflow of refugees; the Southeast Asian states agreed to permit boat people and others to enter and to remain temporarily; and the Western nations agreed that they would resettle the camp populations on a permanent basis. The United States took the lead by announcing, even before the conference, that it was prepared to resettle up to 14,000 persons a month. Others that made major resettlement commitments were Australia, Canada, and France. Virtually every country of Western Europe expressed readiness to offer permanent homes for Indochinese. Japan indicated that it would finance up to one half of the cost of the asylum operation. A vast system for housing and transporting the refugees was established. It involved the UNHCR, the ICM, and many local as well as international voluntary agencies. New camps and new processing centers were built. Special flights began to move refugees out of Southeast Asia toward resettlement countries. Even with that effort, however, it was only in 1980, a year after the Geneva conference, that the number of refugees leaving Thailand exceeded the arrivals.

Refugee resettlement from countries of Southeast Asia was to become the largest organized movement of people since the days of the IRO. More than a million and a half Indochinese have left their homes, most of them for distant continents. More than three-quarters of a million now live in the United States, spread throughout much of the country although with heavy concentrations in California and Texas. Approximately 250,000 have settled in the People's Republic of China. Australia and Canada have each taken in more than 100,000. France has taken almost as many. Smaller but still significant groups have resettled in many other countries of Western Europe, Asia, or Oceania.

Vietnam in 1979 agreed to a special arrangement known as the Orderly Departure Program (ODP) to help spare potential refugees the hazards of flight and to enable persons who had family members already in the West to leave. This program represented a significant innovation because it marked an effort to permit persons who needed or wanted to leave Vietnam to do so without having to run the anguish and the risks of the boat trip. Vietnamese could apply for departure for the United States or for the other Western countries that participate in the program, virtually every country of resettlement. In turn, those countries could indicate which Vietnamese they would be prepared to receive. They could also propose names, often relatives of those already abroad.

The United States had a particular interest in the program because of its involvement in the Vietnam War. It hoped to receive many Vietnamese who had served at the side of the U.S. forces or others who had been government officials and who might be "re-education camp" inmates. Like many other countries, it has also proposed relatives of those who had already settled in the United States. Lists have been exchanged and decisions on departures made. The ICM made the arrangements to fly the persons to the United States. The program has been a significant success.

More than 125,000 persons were able to leave Vietnam by the ODP between 1979 and 1987.

Difficulties have now arisen in the administration of the program, not only for the United States but for other countries as well. Although some persons are still able to leave Vietnam, the Vietnamese authorities have accepted no new names for processing because they wish Western nations first to take more persons from the Vietnamese exit lists. The backlog of earlier applications approved by Vietnam and the United States is shrinking. The program may either grind to a halt by the fall of 1987 or, even if resumed, may not be able to operate at capacity for some time because it will take at least several months for new names to be agreed upon and processed.

The international community also undertook to deal with the pirates who had been preying on refugees in the waters off Indochina. A special antipiracy program has been developed to patrol the waters and to investigate reports of pirate attacks in order to locate and prosecute the culprits. Pirate attacks have not been stopped but there has been some reduction in their number. Dozens of pirates have been seized and sentenced.[74]

The Cambodians

The departure of Cambodian refugees was less publicized than that of the Vietnamese boat people but their flight was at least equally desperate after their country suffered one of the great holocausts of the twentieth century.

In April 1975, as South Vietnam was falling, Khmer Rouge revolutionaries seized power in Cambodia. They were determined to return the country to its essentially rural character. They also wished to erect a radically new socialist society. They emptied the cities, abolished all rights, seized farmers' property and produce, and began a systematic effort to eradicate those elements of Cambodian society that they found unacceptable. More than one million Cambodians were reportedly killed during the three years of Khmer Rouge rule. Hundreds of thousands tried to flee the country. About 150,000 fled into Vietnam, perhaps 10,000 into Laos, and other tens of thousands into Thailand or into the border region near Thailand. Many who were not able to reach safety may have been subsequently executed. Those that reached other countries alive told horrifying stories, many of which were not initially believed, of mass murder in Cambodia.

In 1978, after a long period of deteriorating relations between the two countries, Vietnam invaded Cambodia and installed another government, accelerating the flight West not only of the Khmer Rouge and their leaders but also of others who wanted either to avoid the war or the new regime. By the beginning of 1979, more than 100,000 had fled to the border area near Thailand. The Thai government asked Western states to resettle any Khmer who entered Thailand. When no commitment was forthcoming, the Thai pushed the Cambodians back into Cambodia. Many may have been killed. The Thai authorities continued to restrict access to any Cambodian wishing to enter Thailand, keeping the potential refugee population on the Cambodian side of the border.

With the prospect for resettlement opening after the Geneva conference, the Thai government permitted large-scale entry of the Cambodians in the fall of 1979. Two major camps were opened inside Thailand to hold the new arrivals. One, Khao I Dang, was to become for a time the largest settlement of Khmer in the world. It was a large evenly arranged camp of multiple homes and barracks teeming with refugees, international officials, and voluntary agencies. Another camp, Sakaeo, was smaller and farther from the border. In addition to these camp populations, however, around a quarter of a million Cambodians remained in an area that became known both informally and officially as "the border"—a stretch of land sometimes several miles wide on both sides of the Thai-Cambodian frontier. In that border area, Cambodian nationalist groups and a few international agencies functioned. Relief could be distributed in the border area. It could also be passed to the hungry displaced population in Cambodia itself through a system termed the "land bridge," by which food was trucked into the border area from Thailand and carried off into Cambodia by private persons and families. Many Cambodians hiding in the western portions of their country came to the land bridge at regular intervals to get food for themselves and their families or communities.

In 1980, and particularly in 1981, Western nations began accepting the applications of Cambodians for resettlement. The population of the camps began declining slowly. Sakaeo was closed. The border population also shrank to about 200,000 as many were able and willing to return to their homes in Cambodia. In the spring of 1985, however, a special drive by Vietnamese and Cambodian government forces pushed the border population completely into Thailand. At Thai insistence, that population was – with some exceptions – not permitted to enter Khao I Dang. Instead, it remained immediately on the Thai side of the border, sometimes in new sites. The Thai government has not permitted any others to enter Thailand and has also severely restricted the ability of the Cambodian border population to apply for resettlement so as to preserve a clear distinction between that border population and the Cambodians who had earlier entered Thailand and who still remained at Khao I Dang.

In recent years, the rate of resettlement to the West has fallen. Whereas about 20,000 persons were resettled each year from Khao I Dang in 1984 and 1985, only 6,000 were resettled in 1986.[75] Many Western countries, particularly the United States, have indicated that they are unlikely to accept many more Cambodians for resettlement. They assert that they will not even review pending cases because they have already done so several times. Thousands who have waited in Khao I Dang since 1979 and 1980 have been rejected for resettlement.

The Thai government fears that it may be left with a

residual population of Khmer refugees in Khao I Dang. Because of long-standing ethnic animosities, it does not want such a lasting presence. It has now formally closed Khao I Dang and indicated that the population remaining in the camp would be moved into the temporary sites along the Cambodian border. This represents a particular hazard to the Khao I Dang population because most of its residents have no affiliation with any of the Khmer resistance groups that are active in the border camps. As of this writing in the summer of 1987, the Thai government has not fully carried out its threat, but has started to move some of the camp population to the border area. It remains to be seen whether, as the Thai hope, the threat will act as a spur to accelerated resettlement efforts by Western countries. It also remains to be seen whether the UNHCR will still be able to protect refugees in their new sites on the border.

The Laotians

The situation in Laos evolved differently than that in Vietnam or Cambodia during the climax of the Indochina War in 1975. There was less military activity, no mass invasion, and no major battle. Nonetheless, a significant proportion of the population of Laos has sought refuge.

In 1975, the Pathet Lao resistance movement took power in Vientiane with Vietnamese support. It established the Lao People's Democratic Republic, leading to a rapid acceleration in the departures that had already begun among the ethnic Vietnamese, Chinese, and Thai, as well as among large groups of Laotians and some minority highlanders directly associated with the United States in the Indochina war. Many of those highlanders, often known as the Hmong although the Hmong represent only the largest group, had often fought along with U.S. Special Guerrilla units in Laos, had guided U.S. soldiers, and had saved U.S. pilots who had crashed in Laos. They could not remain in Laos any longer and they were acceptable for resettlement to the United

States. But many were not certain that they wanted to leave their homes forever. They chose Thailand as a place to wait out events in relative safety.

By the end of 1975, more than 25,000 ethnic Lao had fled, as had about 30,000 highlanders. The Laotians had a difficult exodus. They had to cross the Mekong River, which at times is more than half a mile wide and flows very fast during the rainy season. Many of them also became boat people, but their boat was a log on which they paddled themselves and their families across the Mekong, often reaching Thailand miles downstream from where they started, often capsizing and drowning. The highlanders had to cross many miles of virtually impenetrable upland jungle in which they were systematically hunted down by Vietnamese trying to block their escape. Once in Thailand, the Laotians went in different directions. The lowland Lao went into camps such as Nong Khai in the flat valley south of the Mekong River; the highlanders went into separate camps such as Ban Vinai in the green hills of northern Thailand. After the 1979 Geneva conference, more Laotians were accepted for resettlement in the West and the pace of flight into Thailand accelerated.

To discourage further flight from Laos, Thai authorities in 1981 began implementing a plan called "humane deterrence," under which living arrangements for the refugees were made deliberately primitive and resettlement opportunities to the West were denied or sharply curtailed. Thailand placed new lowland Lao arrivals into a specially established "humane deterrence" camp at Na Pho. There, refugees were crowded into facilities well below the standards of other camps in Thailand, with barely adequate sanitary facilities and severe restrictions on movement. No voluntary agencies were permitted to operate in the camp. The policy had some effect, and the outflow of Laotians slowed over the next several years.

In response to requests from Western resettlement nations and agencies, Thailand opened Na Pho in 1984 for resettlement, especially for family members of persons already in the West. The pace of departures from Thailand again began to increase. As it did, so did the inflow from Laos, tripling in 1984 to 19,000. To attempt to stem the flow again, the Thai and Western governments began screening new Laotian arrivals, and those who could not substantiate a claim to refugee status or their prospects for early resettlement could be returned to Laos. The Thai and Western governments arranged that persons so returning would not suffer retribution for having fled. Under this program, about one-third of the several thousand persons who reached Thailand have been told that they would have to return to Laos. The Lao government has so far not accepted any of the persons who have been designated for return. Nonetheless, the rate of flight from Laos into Thailand has slowed significantly. The Thai authorities pushed back Laotian refugees on several highly publicized occasions, at least one of which led to the death of a refugee. These actions may well have contributed to the decline in the arrival rate.

The Laotian refugees have been unique in Indochina because some of them have volunteered to repatriate to Laos and have been accepted. About 3,000 of those have been offered some international assistance to reestablish themselves. Available information indicates that they have not been punished for their escape. Those who repatriated were, however, largely from lowland Laos, not members of the hill tribes who had helped the Americans.[76]

The problem of those Indochinese refugees remaining in Thailand and Southeast Asia is now in numerical terms largely a Laotian problem. Most of the Cambodians and Vietnamese in Thailand have been resettled. Of the 115,000 refugees remaining in Thailand in the spring of 1987, 75 percent are of Laotian origin.[77] Many of them are not certain that they want to resettle in the West, although a large number would probably be eligible to come to the United States because of their close association with the U.S. war effort in Indochina. Many who have come to the United States have had considerable difficulty adjusting to American life. Many may ultimately remain in Thailand, if the

Thai government permits it, without ever being formally admitted for integration, remaining in a kind of legal limbo. A U.S. panel of senior officials that visited Indochina in 1985 suggested that the best solution for the Laotians, especially the highlanders, over the long run might be to remain in Thailand, but it is not clear that the government of Thailand is prepared to accept them.[78]

Beyond the Laotians, many problems remain for all Indochinese refugees. The number of refugees in the camps continues to decline, but at a slower rate than before. It is uncertain what will happen to the Cambodians now in Khao I Dang. It is even more uncertain what will happen to the thousands of Vietnamese scattered in camps and holding centers in Hong Kong, Thailand, Malaysia, Singapore, and Indonesia. Many who have been in camps for years have come to be known as "long-stayers" because of their extended residence in a refugee situation.

The countries of first asylum are increasingly taking steps on their own to solve the problem, at least for themselves, by closing camps, expelling refugees, or denying admission. This trend will continue if no overall solution is found. No one can anticipate when the arrivals will end. A number of asylum countries are even openly speaking of repatriation to Indochina as a solution, although it is clear that this could be a harsh solution for refugees.[79]

For those waiting in camps in Southeast Asia, the questions that remain loom much larger than the answers now offered by both asylum and resettlement countries. They do not know who will take them or when. Many have endured a series of turndowns by resettlement countries, and many have been forced to move from one location to another. None know what the future holds. The only thing that is certain is that they have not volunteered to repatriate to Indochina and that few, if any, could safely do so.

If the Indochinese refugees initiated the current era in refugee reception and assistance a decade ago, they now symbolize its cruel dilemma. Many have lived in camps for more than seven years. Their children may know no other existence. But they still wait, and the longer they wait, the less chance they have of moving on. They demonstrate the sad reality that the world knows how to manage refugee problems but has not yet found a way to solve them.

Africans

For most of the postwar period, Africa has been in turmoil, racked by anticolonial struggles, civil wars, wars between new states, and a host of economic and climatic crises. It has also been, for over 20 years, the continent with the greatest number of countries directly or indirectly affected by the refugee problem. At least four major forces contend in Africa, generating almost perpetual tension and refugee movements. Some of those forces are the special mark of our time, but others may go back generations or longer.

The single most powerful force is nationalism. This force fueled the anticolonial wars that expelled Western nations and their associated hierarchies from most of the nations of the continent. It is doomed, however, to be a perpetually frustrated nationalism because virtually no African state can be a homogeneous nation-state. The borders left by the colonial legacy only rarely conform to national or tribal boundaries. Few of the national groups are sufficiently numerous or powerful to control territory large enough for a truly independent modern state. Those that are large enough are often spread over the territory of several states and cannot form a state of their own without war or flight. Groups that represent a majority in one state may only be a minority in another. Even the most powerful nationalist drives, therefore, can rarely find satisfaction within existing borders.[80]

Another powerful force is the lingering and intensely felt conflict surrounding the apartheid system in South Africa. The existence of this system creates tensions not only within South Africa itself but also across the whole continent, particularly in the states bordering on South Africa. Those states are economically dependent on South Africa and militarily too weak to oppose it. Nonetheless, they find the system abhorrent and want to help those who are there and those who are able to flee.

A third force is the East-West conflict, strongly manifest in some portions of Africa, especially around the Horn and in several states in southern Africa, such as Angola and Mozambique. It mixes with other forces to fuel particularly volatile situations that many African and non-African states view with grave concern.

The last force is the strong drive among African nations to develop their economies. The model for such development is usually the industrial and communications society of the Western world. This model is a particularly difficult one to emulate for societies that have traditionally been agricultural, pastoral, nomadic, and/or commercial, and whose patterns of organization and structure are very different from the West. It is a long and, therefore, frustrating task.

These tensions sometimes reinforce and exacerbate each other, generating considerable pressure and often conflict across or within borders. In the process, they help generate the massive flows of refugees that have characterized the last several decades of African history. It is, in fact, little wonder that Africa has produced and is producing so many refugees, given the immensity of the forces contending across the continent and often within individual countries and societies.

Counteracting these forces and tensions is an extraordinary sense of African brotherhood, an emotion that Africans describe with genuine feeling because it is part of their history and also part of their association forged in reaction to their relations with the white man. For Africans, as for many non-Westerners, personal and communal relations are much more important than the legal relations basic to much of current Western culture. Thus, African refugee streams often tend to move in groups of extended families and communities rather than as individuals, and they are welcomed as such.

The first major African refugee movement in the post-war period was the flight of refugees from Algeria to Morocco and Tunisia during the Algerian civil war in the late 1950s and early 1960s.[81] Those refugees represented the first occasion on which the UNHCR was invited to assist in Africa, both for the care and protection of refugees and for their repatriation in 1962 after the Evian accords ended the Algerian war.

In the next several years, many groups and even whole nations of refugees were to follow. They were driven from their homes by anticolonial, civil, or international conflict, and sometimes by a combination of these. Such conflicts drove refugees from the former Portuguese territories of Angola and Mozambique into Zaire, Zambia, and Botswana; from Guinea-Bissau into Senegal; and from the Republic of South Africa, former Southwest Africa, and former Southern Rhodesia into a whole cluster of other states.[82]

Soon thereafter came those fleeing the complex and often violent process of nation-building in the newly independent states, often representing minority nations within the boundaries of the new states. Such refugees were the Ewe from Ghana, the Hutu and Tutsi from Rwanda and Burundi, the Lampa from Zambia, and the Asians from Uganda. Those groups all settled permanently in other states, usually in Africa, except for the Indians from Uganda who went largely to Great Britain. Others who fled were Eritreans from Ethiopia and a number of southern ethnic and religious groups from Sudan. Most of the latter repatriated after the Addis Ababa agreement of 1972. Smaller groups or individuals sought refuge from other African states as new regimes consolidated their power. By 1972, there were already more than a million refugees in Africa.

As these different groups of refugees fled, particularly from the newly independent states, African leaders became increasingly aware that the refugee presence might become a source of tension among African states. Countries of origin feared that refugees that had gone to a neighboring country might use that country as a base against their former countrymen. Asylum countries feared that the countries of origin might attack them, even when they were harboring refugees for purely humanitarian reasons.

In 1967, African leaders convened a major conference in Addis Ababa to set out the principles by which refugees would be treated in Africa. They wanted to establish a refugee concept appropriate to the African experience and to define the relationships that were to exist between countries of origin and countries of asylum. They knew that the 1951 convention, based on the European experience, was not fully appropriate to Africa because African refugees fled not only persecution but conflict. The Africans also understood that the presence of refugees had not generated the same degree of tension in Europe between countries of origin and countries of asylum as was the case in Africa.

The 1967 conference laid down the principles that were later to find expression in the 1969 OAU convention on refugees. In addition to the wider refugee definition that was to be written into the OAU convention, African leaders agreed that asylum was to be regarded as a humanitarian act, not as a political act reflecting any hostility toward the country of origin. They agreed that countries of origin were to respect that humanitarian act, and countries of asylum in turn would ensure that refugees did not engage in hostile activity against their former state.

Many African governments also wanted to arrive at a principle of burden-sharing. Under that principle, states with a disproportionate number of refugees might be empowered to call on other African states to assist, either by providing relief or by providing additional asylum space. That principle came to be regarded as particularly important by the states in southern and southeastern Africa because it was clear that they would be receiving most of the refugees from South Africa.[83]

The major principles and concepts of the 1967 Addis

Ababa conference not only found expression in the 1969 convention but have also guided the general policies of African governments. They were reinforced by a further conference held in Arusha, Tanzania in 1979.[84] Although there have been some forcible returns or exchanges of refugees in Africa, refugees have generally been treated on a strictly humanitarian basis.[85] Burden-sharing has not always functioned because some of the refugee groups have been so vast that they could not have been moved to asylum in another country, nor would they have wished to go. African countries, however, traditionally grant urgent asylum to refugees who are located in those states, especially around the rim of South Africa, in which the presence of a particular refugee could lead to an attack or a political crisis. Many West African countries have also opened places in their higher level educational system for refugees from southern or East African states to reduce the burden of refugees on educational systems.

Ten years after the OAU convention, the African states realized that refugee flows from independent African states were continuing to increase. Although refugees returned in 1979 and 1980 to newly independent Zimbabwe, they were fleeing in larger numbers into Somalia and Sudan from Ethiopia and other countries. By the beginning of 1979, there were already about 120,000 Ogadeni from Ethiopia in Somalia, fleeing a conflict between the Ethiopian army and Ogaden nationalists who wanted to annex the Ogaden region to Somalia. Two years later, that number had risen to an estimated 700,000 in camps and about the same number scattered among the ethnically similar Somali population throughout towns and rural areas in Somalia. In Sudan, the estimated refugee population from Ethiopia, Zaire, Uganda, and Chad had reached 500,000. The total number of refugees in Africa exceeded 3 million, with little prospect of any early reduction.[86]

These developments meant not only an increased number of refugees for the asylum countries and for the continent but a wholly different type of problem. Refugees fleeing the anticolonial struggles could presumably expect repatriation as soon as their home country was independent. No such assumption could be made about refugees from the independent African countries. The OAU and African asylum countries, as well as the High Commissioner for Refugees, had already drawn such a conclusion, urging settlement of refugees in their countries of asylum as suggested in the OAU convention. With ever growing numbers of refugees, however, it was clear that they would represent a larger and longer-lasting problem for the continent as a whole. African governments especially feared that the refugees would paralyze or at least impede development by diverting or exhausting vital resources.

To deal with this, the OAU, in conjunction with the UN secretary general and the High Commissioner, called an international conference on assistance to refugees in Africa (ICARA I) in Geneva in 1981.[87] The African countries at that conference described their massive needs to the donor community and appealed for help, not only for the refugees themselves but also for the asylum countries increasingly afflicted by the size and the impact of the refugee presence on their territories. Donors took the occasion to announce pledges of $562 million in aid for African refugees. One half of the aid was announced by the United States.

Despite these massive pledges of assistance, many African countries felt disappointed that few new resources were pledged beyond those already scheduled and that none of the support that was provided was earmarked to deal with the particular developmental problems of Africa's asylum countries. They therefore arranged for the convening of another conference (ICARA II) in 1984 to address that particular problem above all others.

Whoever has visited an African refugee camp can understand that the effects of refugee concentrations on asylum countries can be severe. All vegetation for miles around a camp disappears as refugees search for firewood or as their remaining animals graze. Local water supplies are usually exhausted in short order. Roads, worn by relief trucks, lie rutted if not completely destroyed. Even though refugee settlements may have their own schools and clinics, the camp schools rarely go beyond the primary grades and the clinics rarely offer more than basic medical care. For those services, refugees must rely on local facilities, which are usually already overcrowded even before the refugees arrive. Refugee flows can also have severe consequences on those living near the settlements.[88]

The African asylum countries stressed that at ICARA II they particularly hoped for contributions that would help relieve those types of burdens that were caused by refugees or even, on occasion, by returnees.[89] They presented a list and description of projects at the conference in order to attract donor attention. Their needs were met in part by a series of pledges to support many of those projects, but much of the assistance that had been pledged at ICARA II was not in fact given. The immediate reason was that, barely six months after the end of the conference, Africa suffered a devastating drought. Many of the funds that Western donor nations had originally earmarked for ICARA II projects were diverted to help cope with the drought.

The diversion of resources has not, however, been the principal factor inhibiting progress on the concept that underlay ICARA II. Instead, the conceptual breakthroughs have been frustrated by structural and organizational difficulties. The conference attempted to merge economic development assistance with the needs caused by the presence of refugees, but those two subjects are handled by different and sometimes even competing bureaucracies at every level. African governments and donor governments, with rare exceptions, have separate ministries and separate budgetary processes for refugee relief programs and development programs. The two subjects do not merge easily in either the donor or the asylum country, especially because the African development ministries are under an obligation to secure economic development aid for their own people rather than for refugees. This dilemma was reconciled at the conference by agreement that assistance to refugee-related projects should be additional to other development assistance already pledged, but a persistent concern remains that one program might compete with the other rather than supplement it.

The gap between the refugee and development bureaucracies is equally wide at the level of international agencies, whether intergovernmental or voluntary. There has therefore as yet been no satisfactory process for generating a continuing flow of ICARA II projects either in the donor countries or the asylum countries. Some projects have been carried out with funds contributed to the UNHCR or to the UNDP. Others have been carried out through bilateral arrangements between donor and asylum countries. Voluntary agencies have also been involved in some projects and have been very willing supporters of the ICARA II concept.[90] But the concept of ICARA II has not been fully realized to date. Although the conference and the follow-up have been coordinated by a steering committee that includes the UN Secretariat, the OAU, the UNHCR, and the UNDP, coordination has not functioned smoothly and some significant agencies are not fully involved. As one member of the ICARA II steering committee observed, the members of the committee are even not fully informed on the projects that are being undertaken.[91]

To compound Africa's refugee burden since ICARA II, new and sometimes massive flows of refugees have taken place from 1984 to 1987 across virtually every section of the continent. The most dramatic took place during the latter part of 1984 and the beginning of 1985, when a devastating drought hit Africa, particularly the countries around the Horn. Hundreds of thousands streamed into Sudan from Ethiopia and Chad. They presented a grim image of famine. Thousands of persons, particularly children, died of starvation every day until they obtained relief. Despite uncertainties as to whether they were refugees or famine victims or both, the UNHCR played a central role in providing relief for them while they were in Sudan. In the process, considerable quantities of relief supplies also had to be made available to neighboring Sudanese as well as to refugees who had earlier been settled in Sudan but whose harvests had also failed. The United Nations established a major new type of international relief coordination, the Office of Emergency Operations in Africa (OEOA), to cope with the combination of problems.

Even as refugees were being assisted in east and west Sudan, civil conflict in southern Sudan drove many Sudanese into northern Uganda, generating new relief problems. It also closed settlements that had been established for Ugandan refugees in southern Sudan and that were functioning well. At the same time, former refugees were returning to northern Uganda from Zaire.[92] New groups also fled from Ethiopia into a completely new area of Somalia, where emergency camps had to be established to care for them.[93]

The most serious crises arose in southern Africa, where an intensification of the Mozambique civil war after 1985 drove hundreds of thousands from Mozambique into the neighboring countries of Malawi, Zambia, and Zimbabwe, and even into South Africa itself.[94] In addition, tens of thousands of Angolans fled from an expansion of their civil war to find refuge in southeastern Zaire, in the province of Shaba. Others fled into Zambia.[95]

Even as these new flows have been erupting, efforts have been made to repatriate refugees wherever possible. In 1986 and 1987, refugees who had fled to escape the drought in Tigre and Eritrea returned to Ethiopia, generally under the aegis of their own ethnic resistance organizations.[96] In other instances, repatriation from Djibouti, Somalia, and Sudan to Ethiopia has been carried out by the UNHCR in cooperation with the Ethiopian government.[97] Although the High Commissioner has assured himself that the repatriations were voluntary, there has been some renewal of international criticism that refugees were being returned to Ethiopia against their will because the persecution and turmoil from which they had fled had not really ceased.[98]

The experience of the last several decades, especially of

the last several years, suggests that the African refugee problem remains far from a solution. New flows appear frequently, sometimes supplementing old ones but sometimes in entirely new areas. Some settlement programs have been and can be established. But civil war or natural catastrophe can disrupt those, as in the Sudan. The concept of linking refugee aid and development in such a manner as to minimize the burden on asylum countries had been discussed and even agreed upon at ICARA II, but the follow-up has not measured up either to expectations or to needs.

Afghans

Refugees from Afghanistan represent the largest single concentration of refugees in the world today. Most of them, around 3 million, live in Pakistan. Another large number, estimated at between 1.5 and 2 million, live in Iran. Thousands have moved to the West, largely as individuals or in small family groups. The remainder have now been in camps for 7 to 10 years.

The Afghan refugees, like many refugees in history, have fled largely for religious reasons, although many have also fled to avoid the intense warfare in Afghanistan and the hostile government. Like the Huguenots and other religious refugee groups, they have become refugees to preserve their faith and their way of life. Unlike those groups, however, who established themselves permanently in other countries, the overwhelming majority of Afghan refugees are determined to return home at the earliest opportunity.

Afghans in Pakistan

Afghan refugees in Pakistan arrived in a series of waves beginning with small numbers as early as 1973 after the coup against King Zahir Shah in Kabul. Only several hundred came at first, but the number rose to about 80,000 in the next six years and climbed rapidly just before and especially after the Soviet invasion of December 1979. By the end of 1979 they were at the level of 400,000, a number that continued to climb, sometimes at the rate of 3,000 per day, until it reached close to 3 million in 1982. Since then, the figure has remained relatively constant. Some refugees return to Afghanistan for short periods when the fighting abates near their homes. New groups often flee when the war reaches a new area in Afghanistan. As in many African countries, the refugees who live in the camps are mainly farmers, herdsmen, nomads, artisans, merchants, and their families. Many of the middle and upper classes live in Pakistani cities or have moved to the West and, in some instances, have chosen resettlement there.[99]

The refugees have received a generous reception in Pakistan despite their high numbers. They come from a similar ethnic, cultural, and religious background. Like most of the inhabitants of Pakistan's Northwest Frontier Province and Baluchistan, they are Pushtu peoples. They are also accepted under the strongly felt Islamic tradition mandating hospitality to those who need asylum.[100]

Refugees in Pakistan are housed mainly in about 350 camps often located along the border but normally far enough away from it for safety. Because of their large numbers, they dominate many sections of the Northwest Frontier Province. More than a million and a half refugees live in that province, with another 700,000 in Baluchistan, a much smaller number in Punjab, and perhaps 20,000 in Karachi. There are long stretches in western Pakistan where one is never out of sight of a camp when flying over the province by helicopter. Only half a dozen Western voluntary agencies play any role, with the administration performed by Pakistan government agencies employing more than 7,000 people.

As in Indochina, assistance is intended to be temporary. There is a strong emphasis on traditional education because the refugees plan to return home, although some girls do attend school—a sharp break with the past. Relief agencies try to provide enough water and fuel to help refugees without depriving the local population. This has required extensive and separate water systems as well as an elaborate program for providing kerosene and fuel-efficient stoves. When tents proved inadequate for the fierce winters, relief agencies brought in materials with which the refugees have built more traditional huts and walls for their families and livestock. Many of the camps have come to look like Afghan villages, with mud huts and walls high enough to conceal the women as well as the gardens from outsiders' eyes.

Despite these efforts, a number of problems have arisen between the refugee groups and the local population. Those problems can be ascribed mainly to the enormous numbers of refugees, which tend to exhaust local resources rapidly and to overburden the fragile ecology in what was already a relatively barren land. Moreover, refugee men have often moved to towns, especially Quetta, Peshawar, and Karachi, where they compete for employment. Even though the refugee presence has given some boost to the local consumption economy because the refugees spend any allowances that they receive to buy items not in their assistance baskets, the refugees have taken jobs from local residents and have come to dominate such trades as truck transportation and carpet-weaving. Tensions have led to fights and demonstrations but not to any change in the government's basic policy of hospitality.[101]

Such tensions have risen especially since the fall and winter of 1986, as the Soviet Union accompanied its negotiations on Afghanistan with renewed military drives. The Afghan air force bombed camps and border villages, killing Pakistanis as well as Afghans. More Afghans fled from the intensified fighting, with refugees from as far as western Afghanistan appearing at camps in Pakistan. Nonetheless, the Pakistan government has reiterated its determination to continue to offer asylum to the Afghans and there is strong public support for the government's policy.[102]

To help alleviate some of these tensions and to provide

some useful activity for refugees, a new type of assistance project has been started in Pakistan. The World Bank, in conjunction with the UNHCR, has developed some income-generating programs for reforestation and other agricultural activities in the areas of heaviest refugee impact. These often consist of tree plantings in small river valleys and of other efforts to overcome some of the damage caused by the massive refugee presence. The main condition has been that refugees make up at least half the number of employees in the program. Valued at $20 million, the programs have been a considerable success and will continue with a second phase at the level of $40 million starting at some time in 1987 or 1988. They represent a significant innovation that could be usefully transferred to other countries in which refugees need to be employed without competing with local labor and where ecological damage needs to be repaired. Discussions are under way between the UNHCR and the World Bank to initiate similar programs in Somalia and Sudan.

Afghans in Iran

Large numbers of Afghans have fled to Iran. They have settled particularly in the eastern provinces of Khorasan, Kerman, and Sistan-Baluchistan, and to a lesser extent throughout other sections of the country including Tehran itself. The Iranian government estimates that a total of 1.9 million may have arrived, although precise figures are even more difficult than usual to obtain because many came soon after the Soviet invasion when few records were kept and many arrive informally without official clearance. Some have entered Iran through the south, via Pakistan. Out of about 2 million Afghans in Iran, only about 200,000 are in camps. The others live mainly in cities or small towns and are engaged in normal employment.

Afghans have been welcomed in Iran as in Pakistan. In both instances, the refugees are of similar ethnic stock as the people of the border provinces and the Islamic rules of hospitality apply. Many of the refugees in Iran are Shi'ite Muslims and fit well into the Iran population. Moreover, it had been customary for about half a million Afghans to work in Iran even before 1979. Afghans do not attract much notice.[103]

The Iranian government established its own office to care for Afghan refugees in 1979, but for several years did not request international assistance. It finally did so in late 1981. A modest international aid program began in 1983. The principal purpose of the aid is to help with medical screening because many refugees carry diseases such as malaria, cholera, and tuberculosis that had been eradicated in Iran and for which Iranians are neither inoculated nor routinely checked. This has been a particular problem because many refugees travel freely through the country and settle in established towns and villages rather than in camps. One of the objectives of the international aid program is to encourage settlement in designated areas.

Refugees in the Americas

Refugees in the Americas fall essentially into two groups: The first group includes what might be termed the traditional Latin American and even Hispanic refugee, usually fleeing from one Spanish-speaking country to another. These refugees came mainly from urban, middle class, professional, political, or intellectual backgrounds. Such refugees have originated for the most part in South America. Spaniards and, to a lesser degree, Portuguese, also were often part of this particular circuit.

The second group, now much larger in number, are the Caribbean and Central American refugees who came much more strongly into prominence in the 1960s, 1970s, and 1980s. They include not only the same urban professionals but also many workers and peasants. Their fate is linked not only with other Latin American and particularly Central American states but also with the United States and, to a relatively minor extent, with Canada.

The principles governing the protection of refugees in Latin America have found expression in a number of international agreements as well as in the 1951 convention and 1967 protocol, which have been ratified by the majority of Latin American states but not by Brazil or Mexico. Many of the Latin American agreements, such as the 1928 convention of Havana and the 1940 convention of Montevideo, date from the interwar period. These concepts and others were drawn together in the two conventions of Caracas of 1954.[104] The Latin American conventions, as distinct from the global conventions, make a clear distinction between diplomatic and territorial asylum. The former covers those to a diplomatic mission, to a war vessel, or to a military camp or aircraft. The latter covers persons who flee to another country. The two Caracas conventions deal with both of these types.

Both Caracas conventions state that their provisions apply to persons who are being sought for political reasons or offenses but not for civil crimes. The convention on territorial asylum also includes some language drawing on the concepts of the 1951 convention. This underlines that the intent of the nations represented at Caracas was to grant asylum and refugee status to those who fit into the same broad refugee categories as those in the 1951 convention. Other provisions prevent extradition for refugees but also require the asylum states to enjoin refugees from any activities against their homeland.

Although the above provisions for refugees in Latin America enter into the spirit of the international refugee treaties that govern flight from political persecution, such a definition does not fully cover all of the refugees that fled the conflicts in Central America in the late 1970s and the 1980s. A group of senior and mid-level international and Central American government officials, meeting at a colloquium at Cartagena in Colombia during 1984, therefore formulated a declaration that attempted to approximate and even expand for Latin America the principles of the 1969 OAU convention.

According to the Cartagena declaration, the colloquium concluded that it was necessary to consider enlarging the concept of a refugee, "bearing in mind as far as appropriate and in the light of the situation prevailing in the region, the precedent of the OAU Convention . . . and the doctrine employed in the reports of the Inter-American Commission on Human Rights."[105] It recommended that the refugee definition to be used in Central America should include not only refugees covered by the 1951 convention and the 1967 protocol but also persons who have fled "because their lives, safety or freedom have been threatened by generalized violence, foreign aggression, internal conflicts, massive violation of human rights or other circumstances which have seriously disturbed public order."

This definition, by its reference to violations of human rights, went well beyond that of the Caracas conventions and even beyond the OAU convention. It has not been adopted officially by the countries of the region but was cited in a resolution of the General Assembly of the Organization of American States in December 1985.[106] Against the background of current pressures against any further expansion of the refugee definition, it is doubtful that the concept—whatever its merits—can hope to gain global or even regional acceptance in the foreseeable future.

Refugees in South America

This group of refugees fled largely from repressive governments. For Spaniards, that meant the Franco regime, when 20,000 Spaniards became refugees in Mexico and thousands of others sought asylum in other Latin American countries and in a number of European countries as well. Many of these refugees have now returned to Spain, although some did not because of the roots they had developed during their exile years. Similar types of refugees have been exchanged in recent times between a number of Latin

American countries, depending on the character of the government in power. Thousands of persons fled from Argentina during the military regime, but most of those returned after 1983. Many fled from Chile during the years when Salvador Allende was president. Those have largely returned, but even more have fled since the installation of the military regime. Similar refugee flows are part of the history of many other Latin American states, with the refugees generally seeking and finding asylum in other countries of Latin America, in Spain or Portugal, and to a somewhat lesser degree in North American and West European nations.

Caribbean Refugees

The most notable, and largest, Caribbean refugee population has been of Cuban origin. Those who have fled Cuba went largely to the United States but also to Hispanic countries throughout the twentieth century, including during the years when Juan Batista ruled in the 1940s and 1950s. The largest flows began, however, after 1958, when Fidel Castro came to power.[107] A total of more than 1.3 million Cubans have left Cuba in the last 30 years. Most of them have found their way to "little Havana" in Miami, but significant groups have left for Mexico, Spain, and other countries of Latin America and Europe. Those who fled were from virtually all social and economic strata. The professionals, intellectuals, and political figures left first, and other groups followed later.

Many of the Cubans who came to the United States traveled on the basis of arrangements worked out between the United States and Cuba. Often, however, refugees have been the subject of sharp controversy between the two countries. In 1980, the United States government at first encouraged and then opposed an informally arranged and Cuban-sponsored boatlift to Florida from the Cuban port of Mariel.[108] The United States objected most strongly to several thousand criminals and alleged social misfits who were included in the boatlift population. Subsequent attempts to return those persons to Cuba and to arrange for a more orderly process for further Cuban migration to the United States have generally failed because of political tensions between Washington and Havana, although agreement was reportedly within reach several times. In the meantime, the United States as well as other Western and Latin American countries have usually regarded those who fled Cuba as qualified for refugee status – or at least not subject to forcible repatriation.

The other major Caribbean diaspora has been from Haiti, with 1 million – or at least 15 percent of Haiti's total population – living scattered abroad. As with the Cubans, most exiled Haitians are in the United States. The major concentration is about one-half million estimated to live in New York City. An estimated 100,000 or more live in "little Haiti" in Miami. Outside the United States, the largest number are about 300,000 in the Dominican Republic, while other large concentrations can be found in Montreal and the Bahamas.[109]

The exodus from Haiti occurred throughout the rule of François Duvalier but accelerated in the late 1970s. Haitians became another boat people, either leaving their island in their own small vessels, which they beached in Florida, or in larger vessels belonging to professional traffickers who would charge them their life savings and then leave them off along the coast near their ultimate destination. By 1981, the trade had become so extensive that the Bahamas, where Haitians had long performed menial labor, decided to expel 30,000 Haitians as "job-stealers."

In 1981 the U.S. government began to intercept vessels enroute to the United States. U.S. Coast Guard personnel would inquire if there were asylum seekers on board, and the vessels and passengers would then be returned to Haiti.[110] The U.S. government pointed to the miserable economic conditions in Haiti, to the lack of punishment for returnees, and to the heavy involvement of traffickers as evidence that Haitians were coming to the United States for economic reasons rather than out of fear of persecution. The interceptions have been controversial. It is uncertain whether Haitians are given a sufficient opportunity to claim asylum in the quick boat interception, the subsequent interview, and the return to Haiti, particularly as few have done so. Nonetheless, the interception policy is credited with having significantly reduced the flow of boats from Haiti to Florida. Only 6 percent of those Haitians who apply for asylum after reaching the United States, by boat or otherwise, have been granted asylum.[111]

Central Americans

Although the flights from Cuba and Haiti began earlier, it is the different groups of refugees leaving Central American countries that have become the subject of the greatest controversy.

The current problems began in the late 1970s when more than 100,000 persons fled during the Nicaraguan revolution against President Anastasio Somoza. Many of them returned to Nicaragua with the new government of the Sandinistas. Immediately after this, however, violence erupted in El Salvador. During 1980 and 1981, an estimated 250,000 Salvadorans fled, mainly to Honduras, Guatemala, Mexico, and Nicaragua, but with a large though undocumented number coming as far north as the United States.[112] Later, in 1981 and 1982, about 18,000 Miskito Indians from Nicaragua fled to Honduras, and in subsequent years other Nicaraguans came to Honduras and also to Costa Rica. Over the past several years, other large groups have also fled from Guatemala.[113]

By 1986, refugees were scattered over much of Central America, mainly in the following countries:[114]

Honduras. This small country is now the fifth largest recipient of UNHCR funds in the world. There are about 20,000 Salvadorans, 25,000 Miskito Indians, and 6,000 non-Indian Nicaraguans in camps. Another 10,000 Salvadorans are estimated to live outside the camps. Most of the camp refugees live in the lowland or upland jungle in camps that in some instances are very close to the Nicaraguan border. Several thousand refugees have been voluntarily repatriated to Nicaragua and El Salvador. The Honduran government has always wished to keep the camps near the border because it fears that a deeper inland presence might be used to substantiate territorial claims by overpopulated El Salvador and because long-standing animosities between the two countries lead Honduras to regard all Salvadorans with suspicion. Despite its reservations about accepting Salvadorans, however, the Honduran government has permitted refugees to enter its territory and to remain. There have long been rumors that the Nicaraguan opposition recruits among the Miskitos and that the Salvadoran refugees are connected to the resistance there.

There have been efforts to repatriate Salvadorans from Honduras, as mentioned in chapter 3. Some have repatriated by air from Honduras in a program carried out by the ICM. Others have repatriated quietly and without any official recognition. A tripartite repatriation commission of Honduras, El Salvador, and the UNHCR has been formed. There are rumors that other Salvadorans may wish to return from the border camps where they have now been living for 7 years.[115] Some Miskito Indians have repatriated to Nicaragua in response to pledges that the Nicaraguan government would respect their traditional beliefs and customs.[116] Both repatriations have proven controversial. Persons who questioned the safety of life in war-torn El Salvador, as well as those who questioned the human rights policies of the Salvadoran government, have generally opposed repatriation to El Salvador; persons who questioned the good faith and the human rights record of the Sandinista government in Nicaragua generally opposed the repatriation to Nicaragua. The UNHCR in all cases asserted that, as best as could be determined, the repatriation decision had been made voluntarily.

Costa Rica. About 7,000 Salvadorans and 22,000 Nicaraguans are registered as refugees in Costa Rica, with most

Nicaraguans coming during the last year. Camp facilities are being expanded to move more refugees into agricultural environments. Many more Nicaraguans are believed to have entered Costa Rica clandestinely but have not registered as refugees. Many refugees move to the cities to look for employment. Despite its own cramped population and current economic difficulties, Costa Rica has welcomed the refugees in accordance with its long history of hospitality to asylum-seekers, but the large and growing number of unregistered Nicaraguans is generating considerable concern for security as well as economic reasons.

Nicaragua. About 7,000 Salvadorans and 500 Guatemalans have sought refuge in Nicaragua. Refugees live for the most part in established and integrated environments such as agricultural cooperatives rather than in refugee camps. International assistance has been phased down as refugees have integrated more into the local economy. About 600 Salvadorans repatriated voluntarily in 1985.

Mexico. The two principal Central American refugee groups in Mexico are 45,000 Guatemalans and a number of Salvadorans estimated at more than 120,000. The Guatemalans arrived largely in 1982 and 1983 because of military attacks against their villages in the border area. They originally remained in emergency camps near the border itself and did not wish to leave. After an armed attack on one of the camps by Guatemalan forces, however, most of the refugees have now been relocated into camps on Mexico's Yucatan Peninsula, hundreds of miles away from the frontier. Their principal activity is agriculture on land allocated by the Mexican authorities. More than 200 have so far repatriated to Guatemala.

The Salvadoran refugee population in Mexico is less centralized and harder to trace because many have come as individuals and have not formally registered with authorities. Mexican refugee officials estimate that between 120,000 and 150,000 Salvadorans are on their soil, but many unofficial estimates run higher. Most have moved toward such major cities as Mexico City, Veracruz, or Guadalajara. Most look for employment, at least on a temporary basis. Many regard Mexico merely as a transit point for their trip to the United States. They make plans to travel further north at the earliest opportunity. Many establish contact with the clandestine "coyote" network that ferries people into the United States illegally. While in Mexico, they receive assistance if they are formally registered, but only about 4,000 Salvadorans have taken that step. Virtually none have chosen to return to El Salvador.

A whole complex of questions surrounds the future of the refugees in Central America. The political situation in Central America is unsettled and promises to remain so for some time. Refugees represent only one of the problems with which the poor and overburdened countries of the region must try to cope. At the same time they must try to make some progress for their people and avoid being pulled further into a conflict that is playing itself out on their soil but is not fully under their control.

Many countries want to preserve their tradition of hospitality to those seeking asylum but are concerned that the act of giving refuge might pull them into war. Others suspect that refugees are really immigrants trying to abuse their hospitality. The camps, many set only temporarily in the forests and the jungle, often in highland areas not previously opened for agriculture or development, reflect that uncertainty. Like other refugee populations, the Central American refugees are essentially in waiting, with many grave issues still to be resolved before they can even begin to know their fate, much less determine it.

Asylum Seekers in the United States and Canada

Central American refugees have gone north not only to Mexico but also to the United States and, in small numbers, to Canada. Most seek employment there. There has been, as a result, increasing concern about the growing number of Central Americans, particularly Salvadorans, in the United States. It has been informally estimated that Central Americans in the United States (not counting Mexican immigrant laborers) may number more than 1 million, of whom perhaps 300,000 to 500,000 are Salvadorans. They may have come originally for employment as well as to flee various conflicts, but they are now requesting asylum and appealing against deportation.

Their presence has led to confrontations with the U.S. immigration authorities who regard them as illegal migrants. U.S. civil liberties organizations and churches, on the other hand, have strongly supported the right of the asylum seekers to remain, even going to the point of potential illegality in the "Sanctuary" movement, particularly for Salvadorans.[117] There have been many asylum requests, but the approval rates by the U.S. Immigration and Naturalization Service have been low—about 14 percent for Nicaraguans and 6 percent for Salvadorans between June 1983 and September 1986.[118] The U.S. Supreme Court in March 1987 decided that asylum applicants did not have to prove the likelihood of persecution if they were to be repatriated but only that they had a "well-founded" fear, in the words of the 1951 convention and the U.S. Refugee Act of 1980. As of the summer of 1987, the U.S. Congress has before it a bill that would permit Salvadorans and Nicaraguans to remain in the United States under a provision of law granting withholding of deportation, permitting them to remain in the United States until conditions in their home countries can be further investigated to make sure it is safe to return. Such arrangements have already been made for persons from Afghanistan, Ethiopia, Poland, and Uganda.[119]

At the end of 1986, as U.S. authorities began enforcing the new U.S. Immigration Act, a number of Central American asylum seekers began entering Canada. They entered at the rate of several thousand a month, hoping that they could obtain asylum in Canada to avoid the risk that they might be expelled from the United States during the U.S. legalization process. The Canadian government began processing Salvadoran applications, but soon insisted that the applicants remain in the United States during the processing. As a consequence, the number of applications for Canada dropped to several hundred per month.[120]

Washington faces a particular dilemma in dealing with the flow of persons from Central America. The United States has traditionally drawn labor from other countries, and Central American labor has been welcomed in the past. The population increase in Central America is, however, much higher than in the United States and is accelerating proportionately.[121] Large-scale entry for Central American workers would create a labor surplus in the United States competing with U.S. labor for jobs at the lower end of the wage scale. The U.S. government wants to be able to limit the number of immigrants, but could not do so if too many were able to enter because they claimed asylum.

Another problem for the United States is that asylum seekers and refugees have in the past, with some exceptions, not come directly into the United States. The United States has rarely been a country of first asylum. It has generally been a resettlement country, to which refugees might come after they had been screened by U.S. immigration officials in another country. On occasion in the last few decades, in response to such events as the Hungarian uprising or the fall of Saigon, the United States has accepted many more refugees for immigration than could be carefully screened. Most of the time, however, U.S. authorities could carefully review applications before deciding whom to accept. One reason why many Americans reacted sharply to the Mariel exodus was because it appeared that others were determining who would come to the United States. This same reaction supported the interdiction against the Haitians.

Many elements of U.S. public opinion, like the U.S. government, still feel highly uncomfortable with the new role into which the United States has suddenly been thrust. U.S. officials also realize, however, that sudden mass expulsions of Salvadorans or other Central American asylum seekers would have a traumatic impact on the countries of origin because those forced to return could probably not find employment and their countries would lose the foreign exchange that the workers used to remit to their families. President Jose Napoleon Duarte himself appealed to the United States not to expel Salvadorans.[122] President Ronald Reagan has declined the appeal, arguing that few Salvadorans would actually leave.[123] Congressional action may, however, impede large-scale repatriation. Many civil libertarian groups have protested, however, that the U.S. government is less disposed to accept Salvadoran than Nicaraguan asylum seekers because it supports the Salvadoran government but opposes the Nicaraguan.

Europe

Western Europe and North America have always been at the core of the global refugee structure. In part, this was because their publics were strongly sympathetic to those who needed help after each of the two great wars. Most of those refugees were from central and Eastern Europe, peoples akin to the West Europeans in many ways and peoples strongly represented in the U.S. immigrant population. That sense of association undoubtedly played a crucial role in arousing a desire to help.

Refugees from Eastern Europe now rarely generate such emotion, and their movement has become routine in many ways. After the great flood following World War II, the number of East European refugees largely subsided, except for the continuing flight of Germans and some others through Berlin. Immediately after the Hungarian uprising in 1956 there was an upsurge. Many East Germans continued to pour across the sector boundary in Berlin until the Wall was built in 1961. In 1968, a number of Czechs came to the West, but their number was not as high as that of the Hungarians in 1956. When martial law was declared in Poland in December 1981, more than 50,000 Poles were believed to be outside the country. Several tens of thousands then fled Poland, but not all of them sought refugee status and many have since returned.[124]

Refugees still leave Eastern Europe, although in smaller numbers. In 1985, the most recent year for which statistics are now available, the following estimates of departures were made: from Bulgaria, fewer than 1,000; Czechoslovakia, several thousand; Hungary, perhaps 2,000; Poland, the largest group, with estimates in the tens of thousands; Romania, the next largest, perhaps 15,000–20,000; the Soviet Union, close to 2,000. East Germans are not counted as refugees in these statistics because they are accepted as fellow Germans in West Germany.[125]

Precise numbers are difficult to calculate because East-West travel in Europe is not as restricted as it once was and because many—including some of those included in the above statistics—leave for the West as migrants, not as refugees. Many East Europeans may travel to the West as tourists and some choose to remain for some time or indefinitely. They may never formally declare themselves to be refuges. They may later return home. Western authorities, especially in Western Europe, are also more reluctant than in the past to accept unquestioningly that any person leaving Eastern Europe must be granted refugee status because many may come for economic or family reasons without a genuine fear of persecution.

Although many European countries cover their own costs for refugee arrivals, the UNHCR also finances some programs to receive refugees in transit camps and, if appropriate, to help settle them in transit countries. It and the ICM assist in moving refugees quickly westward from transit countries if that is necessary. In addition, the UNHCR runs modest programs in several European countries to help refugees become settled. It also helps in the case of persons who wish to repatriate.[126]

The countries of Europe and North America have also offered resettlement opportunities to vast numbers of refugees from every corner of the world. Because those persons nominally retain refugee status until they are fully integrated, several Western countries have significant refugee populations. It was estimated that, as of January 1, 1986, the United States housed 1 million refugees; Canada, 353,000; France, 174,200; Great Britain, 135,000; and West Germany, 134,000.[127]

A particular interest of the United States has been the emigration of Jews from the Soviet Union. This emigration was agreed upon in the early 1970s as part of the U.S.-Soviet detente. Under those arrangements, hundreds of thousands of Jews as well as some other minorities have been able to leave the Soviet Union, reaching a peak annual level of 51,000 in 1979. As U.S.-Soviet relations cooled, the rate of emigration dropped, to 1,140 in 1985 and 914 in 1986.[128] Although many of the Jews leaving Russia originally state that they plan to go to Israel and receive their emigration documents on that basis, a majority elect to come to the United States once they reach Vienna. They are counted as refugees in the United States and receive refugee benefits. This has recently been of concern to the Israeli government, which has asked that Jews who leave the Soviet Union go to Israel.[129] The issue has gained some urgency because there is widespread hope that Moscow will again permit large-scale Jewish emigration, starting with perhaps 10,000 or more in 1987. The Soviet authorities granted almost 2,000 exit visas to Jews in the first three months of 1987.[130] Press reports also indicate that the Soviet government has agreed that the persons leaving the Soviet Union will be sent to Romania instead of Austria to decrease the likelihood that they will go to the United States, but there are also reports that many might still decide to leave for the United States even after they have arrived in Israel itself.[131] It is uncertain what levels of Jewish emigration might be permitted to other countries, such as Canada, Austria, or France, all of which have a considerable interest and to which Jewish emigration from the Soviet Union has declined significantly since 1980.

* * * *

The refugees described above have been labeled traditional because they have for the most part followed the pattern of flight, protection, and assistance that has become customary since the 1940s. In one important way, however, most of them are not traditional. They are still in place, in their first asylum sites, and have not found a permanent home.

In some instances, as with the Afghans, the refugees have not sought a new home and would not accept one. In other cases, such as the nomadic refugees in Somalia, they may at times even now return to some of their old trails when it is safe to do so. But in most instances, the refugees must wait, either until the problems that forced them to seek refuge are solved or until some other arrangements can be made that will permit them to resume at least some semblance of normal life.

6

The Jet People

The latest class of refugees does not travel as refugees used to do, on foot, by rail, or by boat. It travels by intercontinental jet. Such refugees might start their trip in Kuala Lumpur and continue through Singapore, Bombay, Ankara, Belgrade, Prague, and Berlin, before leaving the air route to travel the next few miles by rail or bus. But their purpose, whatever may be written on the visas – if they have visas – is not traditional tourism. It is to seek asylum.

The Intercontinental Refugees

These new jet people have come largely to Western Europe, although some have also found their way to North America. They have come mainly from Asia and Africa. They sometimes come by highly tortuous routes. They request asylum as refugees once they have arrived in a Western country. The technical refugee literature terms their travel an "irregular movement," because they have already found asylum in one country before traveling on to a second without having obtained permission from the second in advance. In the countries in which they seek asylum, they are often simply labelled illegal immigrants.[132]

The movement began in the 1980s as generosity to refugees became more widely known, as camp situations began to stagnate, and as conditions in some of the countries of origin deteriorated because of war, insurrection, repression, economic misery, or some combination of these factors. Tens of thousands came to Western Europe every year between 1984 and 1986. A particular group of jet people, the Tamils of Sri Lanka, traveled in large numbers from Colombo, New Delhi, Singapore, or Kuala Lumpur to Schoenefeld airport near East Berlin. There they obtained East German transit visas, if they had not already received them with their tickets, and they used these visas to travel either to East Berlin or to the Baltic Sea ferry terminals. If they went to East Berlin, they then crossed the sector boundaries into West Berlin, taking advantage of the lack of border controls because the West regards Berlin as one city. They then requested asylum in West Berlin or in West Germany. If they went to the Baltic, they took a ferry either to Sweden or Denmark and requested asylum there. Many destroyed or jettisoned their passports and visas during the ferry ride to support their claim that, as refugees, they had been deprived of documentation.

Other processes were less complicated. Asylum seekers from Ghana simply flew British Airways to London. Ethiopians entered Europe on a flight to Rome before traveling on by air or land to Switzerland or some other West European country. Afghans came via Karachi and Amsterdam. Iranians, who had a more complex route to follow, entered Turkey on foot across the mountains and then, after obtaining new documentation and tickets at Ankara or Istanbul, flew to any of the major European airports. Many did not even fly to the country of final destination marked on their tickets but got off the aircraft at any suitable transit airport and requested asylum there. Others, such as Iraqis, Palestinians from Lebanon, or Turks, might come by way of Cyprus.

The wave of asylum applicants hit Western Europe like a shock. The continent had seen an upsurge of asylum applicants around 1980 and 1981 because of the Polish crisis, the eruption of refugee flows in several parts of the world, and because many foreign workers who had lost their jobs in Europe during the recession claimed asylum to avoid deportation. By 1983, however, the figure for asylum seekers in Europe had sunk to 69,000, a quantity regarded as tolerable and that, in any case, included the traditional flow of refugees from eastern Europe. Over the next few years, however, the figure tripled, to 103,000 in 1984, 170,000 in 1985, and an estimated 200,000 in 1986.

Some countries found the rate of asylum applicants rising at an even faster rate. In Norway and Denmark, the number multiplied by a factor of 10 between 1983 and 1986, from 200 to 2,700 and from 800 to 9,300 respectively. The number quintupled in Germany, from 19,700 to 96,500, and in Sweden, from 3,000 to 15,000. It quadrupled in Turkey, from 1,200 to almost 5,000, although asylum seekers in Turkey — mainly Iranians — did not usually seek formal asylum there but remained in an informal status while they got ready to move on. Because virtually every European country already had a backlog of unprocessed applications and because each application needed individual attention, the new arrivals threatened to overwhelm processing offices and facilities.

Many of the asylum seekers have been young and single men in their teens, twenties, or thirties. To the skeptical West European immigration authorities, they have looked very much like job seekers or draft evaders who were taking advantage of disrupted conditions in their home countries to legitimize a spurious asylum claim for the purpose of privileged migration. Those immigration authorities have cited traditional refugee doctrine denying refugee status to draft dodgers, except for genuine conscientious objectors, and to job hunters, whom they term "economic refugees."

It did not help the young asylum applicants that they often bought their tickets and perhaps even documentation from black marketeers who were well established and known traffickers regarded with deep suspicion in the West.

It also did not help their claims that, unlike the image of traditional refugees, they did not appear exhausted and tattered after an arduous trek but were usually cleanly dressed, relatively unscathed, and suffering no worse perceptible affliction than jet lag. Although refugee status does not depend on the hazards of one's journey but on the conditions that one flees, the plain fact was that the new arrivals did not fit the image of refugees for which persons in the West had acquired a sense of sympathy.

Over the decades since World War II, Europeans states have promulgated a series of measures intended to welcome persons in need of asylum. Those measures have facilitated entry and eased the transition by offering free lodging, free meals, work permits – at least in some West European countries – and an asylum procedure that was painstaking, generous, lengthy, and replete with possibilities for appeal against any negative decision. The Council of Europe has established a special working level committee to coordinate rules and policies with respect to refugee and asylum questions.

Various institutions of the Council of Europe have also issued several recommendations to governments proposing liberal principles for the treatment of refugees. In 1961, the Consultative Assembly of the Council of Europe expressed the view that it was desirable for member states to confer upon political refugees the right to seek, *receive*, and enjoy asylum.[133] In 1967, the Committee of Ministers recommended that governments should act "in a particularly liberal and humanitarian spirit in relations to persons who seek asylum." It recommended that governments should take no measure, including refusal of admission at the frontier, if such measures would expose a person to the danger of persecution.[134]

The Europeans believed that the new asylum seekers did not really need asylum at all but had come with the cynical intent of taking advantage of all the favorable principles and benefits that had been designed for people in genuine need. Nonetheless, the applicants could often point to certain conditions in their home countries, such as a measure of repression or domestic strife, that could at least justify a case. In some instances, they were also self-created refugees, persons who were not in jeopardy before their departure but who might be harmed upon their return if their governments learned that they had fled to seek asylum and perhaps to escape military service.

Decisions became difficult to make under these contradictory pressures. The rate of asylum approvals fell, often to a level of only one approved application in 10 or more, but this did not always mean that the applicants would return home. Many asylum seekers had submitted applications in more than one country. If they were rejected in one, they would continue to try in another. Some countries, like Germany and France, were known not to escort rejected asylum seekers to the frontier to expel them. Many applicants would ignore a negative decision and would remain in the West, sometimes even in the country in which they had been rejected, scraping together enough odd jobs for a bare existence in the large immigrant communities that have come to exist in such major European cities as London, Paris, Berlin, Amsterdam, or Brussels. Although the illegal worker population in Europe is not at the same level as in the United States, it is still estimated at perhaps 10 to 15 percent of all foreign workers, thus perhaps amounting to 1 million, a number in which there would be ample opportunity to hide.[135]

The existence of these underground communities, however, made the authorities even more determined to find a solution to the problem. Whatever the merits of their suspicions about the real purpose of the asylum seekers may have been, the European states by 1986 and 1987 began taking strong action to impede their further entry.

European countries began revising their laws and regulations regarding treatment of asylum applicants. By the summer of 1987, a number of states had taken such steps or were urgently considering them. The Federal Republic of

Germany introduced new and stiffer regulations at the beginning of 1987, and many voices were even raised to ask for an amendment in the Basic Law that commits the Federal Republic to a generous asylum policy. In Switzerland, a new and firmer asylum law was approved by a margin of almost two to one in a referendum on April 6, 1987. Denmark, long known for its generous asylum policy, also introduced new and stricter regulations. Belgium withdrew from the UNHCR the long-standing authority to make asylum decisions on Belgium's behalf. Other states were under great pressure to follow suit because they were being swamped by asylum seekers looking for the few remaining open doors, and many states were in fact changing their rules in 1986 and 1987.

As part of the new procedures, sometimes preceding them, West European countries began taking steps to deny even physical access to their borders. Several countries, including Germany, Great Britain, and Denmark, insisted that persons from the countries from which most asylum seekers originated could not even enter the country temporarily without a visa. Strictly interpreted, as it usually was, this meant that a Sri Lankan businessman traveling to London could not fly via Frankfurt or Copenhagen airport without obtaining a transit visa for Germany or Denmark in advance.

Several countries established special procedures under which persons who might have reached their airports or border posts would not be legally considered to be on their sovereign territory. They could then be expelled without the necessity of a specific expulsion order. Switzerland created a new special "international zone" around Cointrin Airport in Geneva; asylum seekers could be kept in that zone without being legally in Switzerland. Belgium also introduced special procedures at Brussels airport. In a number of countries, even if applicants were permitted entry, they would be kept under strict detention while their applications were being studied so as to make sure that they could not escape should their application be denied. In some countries, their applications would not be accepted unless they certified that they had not placed similar applications elsewhere.

Denmark, Sweden, and the Federal Republic of Germany made separate agreements with the German Democratic Republic to block the entry of Tamils, Iranians, and others who had been entering Europe through Schoenefeld airport. Under the new agreements, the East German government no longer permitted persons to fly to Schoenefeld and pass through East German territory to the West unless they already had visas permitting them to enter a Western country. Ferry companies also agreed to sequester the documentation of persons traveling to Denmark and Sweden and to give that documentation directly to the Scandinavian authorities so that the passengers could not destroy it in transit.

The West European countries began using airlines to help enforce the stricter rules. Great Britain imposed a fine of £1,000 on any airline bringing in a foreigner who either lacked documentation or was carrying false documentation. Others took similar steps. Several countries insisted that airlines verify travelers' return flight tickets and documentation. They also required that airlines hold a certain number of reserved seats open for undocumented or ill-documented passengers who might need to be sent out of the country immediately.

European countries, including Austria, Great Britain, Sweden, Switzerland, and others, began expelling asylum seekers whose applications had been denied. In some instances they returned the asylum seekers directly to their home country. In others, they sent them to some country through which those seeking asylum had already passed, often Turkey. These expulsions led to suicides in Berlin and Geneva and to traumatic airport scenes in which rejected asylum applicants sometimes wounded themselves to avoid expulsion, scuffled with police and airline personnel if they were forced to board an aircraft, and in one instance, at Heathrow airport in London, stripped to their underpants in protest. Last-minute appeals sometimes delayed departing aircraft and gave the asylum seekers another reprieve and perhaps permission to remain.

The new restrictions had a significant initial impact on the arrival of refugees and asylum seekers. In Britain, arrivals at Heathrow airport were dramatically reduced.[136] In West Germany, similar decreases were reported during the last months of 1986 after the institution of visa requirements for Schoenefeld airport; by February 1987 the rate of arrivals in West Germany had again risen to 5,000 per month, but it subsequently declined again.[137] Reports of decreases in asylum applications came from other European countries, especially from those that had taken stiff measures, but there was also concern that asylum seekers would find new ways to enter.

Although it appeared clear, as in the Swiss referendum, that many citizens of European countries were turning against asylum seekers, a number of powerful groups as well as significant elements of public opinion supported and assisted them. Churches, paralleling the Sanctuary movement in the United States, helped lodge and protect asylum seekers against the authorities. Humanitarian organizations spoke up for them and provided legal advice. Supporters sometimes came to airports to help block expulsions.

The High Commissioner has insisted that even persons who might not qualify under the strict terms of the 1951 definition should at least not be sent home. High Commissioner Poul Hartling convened special consultations on "Xenophobia" and on "Asylum in Europe" in 1984 and 1985. He called for persons who might not qualify under the strict interpretation of the 1951 convention at least to be "protected against forcible return to danger" and for their "minimum human needs" to be met "pending a clarification of the conditions in their countries of origin."[138] He laid particular stress on the persons "of his concern," a formulation that went back to the early days of the mandate refugees. A similar but somewhat wider-ranging position was taken by his successor, Jean-Pierre Hocké, who told the UNHCR Executive Committee in October 1986 that he could not "stand back and cite the convention" when "conflict and violence were identified as being an important factor in the decision to flee."[139] Later, in a lecture at Oxford University, he spoke of "extra-convention" refugees who had to be given the necessary time before returning home even if they did not meet the 1951 definition.[140]

The European countries also engaged in a series of consultations with each other and with the High Commissioner to find a common solution to these problems. After meeting in Stockholm and the Hague in 1985 and 1986, they met with the High Commissioner at Gerzensee in Switzerland in February 1987. The countries represented included Austria, Belgium, Canada, Denmark, France, Germany, Great Britain, the Netherlands, Norway, Sweden, and Australia (as an observer). The meeting, like others before it, served not to make decisions but to exchange information and to consult. Among the issues considered were better exchanges of information on conditions in the countries of origin and the possibility of arrangements whereby asylum-seekers might be returned to countries of first asylum and supported there. This new concept, if agreed, would permit West European states to return rejected asylum seekers to Turkey, Pakistan, or other countries of first asylum, in exchange for assistance in helping to meet the refugees' needs in those countries. The next consultative group was scheduled to be held in the summer or fall of 1987 in Oslo, but the existence of the group clearly did not impede the whole range of separate actions already being taken by individual countries.[141]

European Community members also met among themselves during 1986 and 1987 at the ministerial and the senior working level to try to formulate a common position. They were seeking agreement on a common European visa and travel regime that would be instituted in 1992 and that they hoped would include Austria, Norway, Sweden, and Switzerland as well. Under that regime, any visitor to any West European country could only enter with a common European visa specifically designed to prevent persons from arriving undocumented or ill-documented at any European airport or border. It was uncertain, however, whether the European countries could actually agree on such a general visa regime. France, Germany, and the Benelux countries were also considering a common travel regime for their particular countries. The mood in all European countries was so hostile to asylum seekers and the pressures for agreement so strong that there was a risk that any international standard would be set at the level of the most restrictive country rather than at a more generous level.

The word that crept increasingly into the European dialogue with respect to asylum seekers was the word "regionalization." Under this concept, each region of the world would be responsible for solving its own refugee problems. Western Europe would give asylum to persons from Eastern Europe, but countries in other parts of the world would be the principal agents in solving the problems of their particular regions. This concept represented a striking reversal from the decisions 20 years earlier to universalize the refugee convention through the 1967 protocol. It also went directly against the entire concept of a global refugee structure as it had grown and functioned successfully during the great refugee crises of four decades. The jet people of the 1980s might become the first group of refugees and asylum seekers since World War II whose flight would lead to greater restrictions against refugees instead of toward *greater generosity.

The doors for asylum seekers from the Third World were clanging shut all over Europe during 1986 and 1987. It was not only difficult to obtain asylum, it was becoming increasingly difficult even to reach the point at which an application could be made.

Concepts at Issue

The new situation raises a host of conceptual issues basic to refugee protection and assistance.

Who is a Refugee?

The world has lived with several complementary concepts and definitions of refugees for a number of decades. The European countries and other industrialized states generally apply to asylum seekers the 1951 definition, fully grounded in international humanitarian law. It is also often written into their own laws. There has, however, been a general consensus that the OAU definition was appropriate to the developing world, often even outside Africa, because of the many problems of nation-building, and that the High Commissioner's mandate for other groups of his concern should be respected. The worldwide public image of a refugee has in recent years come to be more identified with the OAU definition than with the convention definition.

Contradictions between these concepts did not arise because persons moving from the Third World to industrialized states would be personally screened by the latter as part of the resettlement process. The irregular movements, in by-passing that process, created a clash in the application of the two definitions and also created a backlash because the Europeans, like the Americans and Canadians, did not regard themselves as countries of first asylum for everyone. They were prepared to assist refugees elsewhere but not to welcome them without careful review.

There was also genuine doubt as to whether the persons claiming asylum as victims of conflict should be granted refugee status. They were often described as "humanitarian" cases, persons who did not flee specific persecution threats but generalized violence, and whom it might be a humanitarian act to accept at least for a short-term residence while matters in their countries of origin might stabilize. But they were not regarded as convention refugees and were often denied asylum. There was no consistency on this matter among various European countries and no common base of information on which to determine what might be the proper course.

Status in the Asylum State

Although immigration asylum authorities in the European states (as in North America) refuse asylum if they do not find the claim justified on the basis of the 1951 definition, the asylum seekers and their supporters argue that even those persons who are not convention refugees should at least not be forcibly returned.

The result is often a stand-off. Athough the applicant's request for asylum is formally rejected, the person may not be returned to the country of origin and may not even be expelled. The applicant may be accorded a status that has been defined in many terms: "B status," "de facto refugee status," or "non-status."[142] The latter term may be the most accurate of all because the person has few rights and essentially descends into a shadow world. In some countries, he is to await a change in conditions in the country of origin; in others, he is to await further review at an undetermined date. Many persons choose to go to another European country or may even be obliged to do so. They usually do not return home if they can avoid it. They may become "refugees in orbit," applying in several countries (sometimes simultaneously), raising the European-wide statistics on asylum applicants to alarming levels because at least 20 percent of the asylum applications in Western Europe have been informally estimated to be duplicate applications. Many remain in the country in which their application was rejected, swelling the ranks of those who live beneath the surface of Western society. In a legal sense, they may have not entered the asylum country; in reality, they may have not left it. Many asylum seekers, whatever their original motive for leaving their home country, are nonetheless prepared to accept "non-status" because it gives them time to establish themselves and because it may seem safer than what they left behind.

The Ethnic Issue

Only two Western societies, Canada and Australia, are among the 20 countries with the highest ratio of refugees per capita.[143] No European country is on that list. Yet it is the European countries, those who are at the foundation of the international refugee structure, who are reacting with such intense concern to a flow of persons dwarfed by the number that may enter Sudan or Pakistan in a single season.

Rightly or wrongly, the charge of "xenophobia" is raised, as it was during the 1984 seminar in Geneva.[144] Participants at that seminar and other voices since then have asked whether the West Europeans, who were so ready to grant asylum to large numbers of their fellow-Europeans, are now closing their borders because the new groups are ethnically different. This is a somewhat different charge from the one made by the Sanctuary groups and others in the United States, who assert that the U.S. asylum policy is determined by U.S. political attitudes toward countries of origin, especially in Central America but elsewhere as well.[145] The ethnic charge is a troubling assertion. If the concept of a global refugee protection and support structure is to retain any real meaning, there can be no apartheid of asylum.

Structural Concerns

The arguments about first asylum can have an impact on the entire global refugee structure, especially if the ethnic argument appears to have merit. One cannot expect countries everywhere to maintain generous asylum policies if they see the European and North American states appear to waver in their commitment. First asylum countries harboring Indochinese refugees in Southeast Asia are already reacting to the situation in the industrialized countries, beginning to tighten their own procedures, turning more people back at the border, threatening to close camps, and moving away from the largely generous policies that prevailed over most of the past dozen years. Although they appear to be tightening up primarily because of lagging Western resettlement, they must also be sensitive to apparent Western departures from the principles on which the entire system has long been based, principles that the West urged on them in the mid-1970s when the boat people began to flee. Even in Africa, where countries have been most generous in opening their doors to refugees, doubts are rising and conditions are hardening.

Which is the Country of First Asylum?

An important legal and technical question has also arisen from the European asylum dispute: Which is the country of first asylum for any refugee or group of refugees? Some European countries have been rejecting applicants by saying that they could have, and should have, applied for asylum in other countries rather than coming to Western Europe. The concept of irregular movement is based on the notion that a refugee has been granted asylum in one country and therefore has no reason to travel further to another. Travel to Germany by an Iranian who has already been granted asylum in Turkey would constitute such an irregular movement. In most instances, however, Third World asylum seekers do not file any formal asylum applications until they enter Western Europe, even if they have passed one or more countries on the way to their chosen asylum country – especially if their transit is only an airport stop. If it is now accepted, as at least some European countries state, that any stop in any country or airport en route should be regarded as the equivalent of an asylum grant or at least as an opportunity to request asylum, it would make every refugee movement past the first stop "irregular" and, by implication, improper travel. It would place an unbearably heavy human and political load on the states contiguous to any country suffering an exodus and could almost compel them to return refugees forcibly. The tightening of rules in one group of states would work its way back through another and would ultimately stifle refuge.

Access and Process: the Question of Control

The refugee flow has raised in Europe the same questions about border control raised in the United States in 1980 and 1981 by the arrival of the Mariel Cubans and the Haitian boat people. Just as the United States then reacted by stopping the Mariel boat flotilla and by interdicting boats coming from Haiti, the West Europeans have now reacted by preventing persons from reaching their national territories.

Once an asylum applicant enters the United States, Canada, or virtually any West European country, it is very difficult to compel the applicant to leave except at considerable expense and after long delay. The process for granting asylum has become so lengthy and so complicated that it can take years for a final decision to be reached. Any energetic asylum applicant can by then have established enough links, either by employment or marriage, that he or she cannot be forced to leave.

This is a case in which the best is the enemy of the good. By devising such a generous and complex process, the Western world now feels compelled to deny access to that process. Potential asylum applicants are stopped at borders because they cannot be permitted even to apply for asylum. If they do enter, they may often be detained so that they can not receive the welfare benefits that may have become an attraction and so that they cannot establish the links that could enable them to stay on should their application for asylum be denied. They may also be detained so that, if they are to be deported, they cannot disappear between the time of the decision for deportation and its date of implementation. But detention, like refusal of access, raises some troubling legal and moral issues. The problem lies not, as is often said, in Western states' control over their borders. Those are relatively easy to control, at least at airports, train stations, or highway border crossings. The problem lies in the control that those states can, or cannot, exercise over persons who have actually entered their territory and in procedures that may not be appropriate any longer.

The intensified border controls and stoppages pose serious risks. They may turn back genuine refugees or even prevent them from fleeing their countries. They may also create some resentment among businessmen and other legitimate travelers from the Third World who will question whether the procedures reflect an ethnic bias, especially if (as reportedly happens on some occasions) they see only Third World travelers being stopped and checked. They may also be against the letter and the spirit of agreements reached among the Europeans themselves in the Council of Europe as well as among members of the UNHCR Executive Committee.[146]

The strict new measures also raise the problem of a competition to raise barriers. When the mood turns against asylum applicants and countries begin closing their borders, it is to the advantage of every state to introduce restrictions before others do. The state that remains generous longest will have the biggest burden. Therefore, once negative steps are introduced, their introduction and their severity tend to accelerate. The process becomes very difficult to arrest and virtually impossible to reverse.

The danger in these arrangements is that there could be two classes of refugees, those that have access to the West and those who do not. The High Commissioner could become an agent for maintaining limited protection in the Third World countries, while also becoming yet another international assistance organization running programs ad infinitum in those countries. Sooner or later, unless North-South bridges are established and opened, the system will have lost the global character that gave it its moral foundation and strength.

Migration Link

Anyone who has walked down the Champs-Elysees, Oxford Street, the Quai du Mont-Blanc, or the Kurfuerstendamm during the 1950s, 1960s, and 1980s sees how things have changed. Then, one heard mainly French, German, or English, with perhaps an occasional sentence or two of Spanish. Europeans and a few North Americans were strolling along, looking at shops and cafes, idly shopping, or just relaxing. Now, one sees a mix of races, hears a babel of tongues, and cannot help but notice that the population of many European cities, like that of many U.S. cities, is evolving toward a polyglot society.

One of the broad refugee developments of this particular decade is the growing link between the new refugee movements and the whole pattern of global migration from south to north. Over the past 40 years, millions of southern workers and migrants have moved north because they needed to find work and because the North needed labor. Virtually every industrialized country now needs immigration or temporary foreign workers to prevent labor force shortages, especially in its traditional industries, in agriculture, and in some service sectors. The South, for its part, has had a higher birthrate and could not offer enough economic opportunity for all its people.

The arrangement worked to the benefit of all concerned. The countries of Europe and North America received the labor force that they required in industries in which their own citizens were often reluctant to work. The other countries saw employment opportunities for their people and stood to benefit from the funds that the workers could remit to their families at home. This kind of labor transfer may well have to continue if the economies of all the countries concerned are to prosper in the future. It is a by-product of the global economy and the global technology. It cannot be reversed.

The merging of refugee, worker, and migrant flows has only begun over the last few years. Before then, refugees from the developing world, despite the rapid growth in their numbers, largely remained in countries of first asylum in the South. Now they evidently no longer wish to do so. New groups that are not yet even recognized as refugees, and perhaps may never be, are coming directly to the North as migrants have done for decades. The full consequences of this are not yet evident and certainly not yet understood. As the world passes further into the jet age and into the global information era, decisions that affect any single element in the new and complex web will need to be carefully considered in the light of their impact on the whole.

7

Conclusions and Recommendations

The list of refugee crises presented in the previous two chapters offers a somber picture. Refugees are everywhere – a by-product of every crisis. But if their creation requires no special effort, finding solutions to their plight certainly does.

There are some hopeful signs. If rumors of a possible political settlement over Afghanistan prove to be correct, large numbers of Afghan refugees can be expected to repatriate. The world refugee total would then be reduced by perhaps one-quarter to one-third.

Another hopeful sign is the growing international concern about the causes of refugee flows. One expression of this is a study by Sadruddin Aga Khan on mass exodus.[147] The Independent Commission on International Humanitarian Issues is following this with studies of its own on the causes of this exodus. If should lead to proposals for prevention.

Another move was initiated in 1980 by the Federal Republic of Germany and passed as a UN General Assembly resolution in 1986. That resolution provides for member states of the United Nations as well as the secretary general to take certain steps to help avert refugee flows in the event of a crisis.[148]

These processes reflect deepening international concern about the global refugee situation and about the way in which potential refugee flights and other large population movements have not to date been adequately weighed in national policy deliberations. It remains to be seen if refugee flows can be prevented, but an effort clearly deserves to be made.

Nonetheless, any realistic assessment must now conclude that refugee movements will continue to be an element of international affairs. Refugees are usually produced by nations in turmoil or at war, and turmoil as well as war can certainly be expected to continue. The process of nation-building in the Third World, especially in Africa, will go on. So will international tension and conflict. So will the growing trend toward the intermingling of refugee, worker, and migration streams, because grim political and economic conditions all too often parallel and amplify each other.

The world may ultimately see a kind of colonization in reverse, from South to North, from developing to industrialized economies, and from overpopulated to underpopulated societies. Refugees may increasingly become a part of this, as economic and political crises occur simultaneously in different countries of the developing world.

Beyond the prosperous and liberal societies of a handful of fortunate industrialized or industrializing states, most nations and peoples around the globe live in immensely fragile situations. One can, therefore, sadly predict that refugees will keep appearing, even if one cannot predict where or when.

In the face of this prospect, the international objective must be to find solutions to refugee problems, or at least to move toward solutions wherever possible. This means a special effort not just to protect and assist refugees but to enable them to find new lives.

The following principles should be the basis for action:

- To redouble efforts at finding long-term solutions,

especially for those who have been in refugee situations for many years.

- To offer asylum to those who need it but not to tempt those who do not.
- To support the countries of first asylum, whose continuing generosity is essential to the functioning of the entire refugee structure.
- To make certain that no state or group of states carries more than its fair share of the burden.
- To address issues in a coordinated way so that policy decisions are made in the same overall framework.
- To preserve the basic elements of refugee protection and care from stagnation, neglect, or abuse.

On the basis of these principles, the international community must specifically attempt to find solutions in two key areas: first, for the long-stayers and the developing countries in which many have found haven; second, for the new intercontinental asylum seekers. Even if definitive solutions cannot be reached immediately, a more conscious process of seeking solutions must begin.

For Long-Stayers

The extended exile of many refugees has now continued for almost a decade. They are weary of their long displacement. Ten years is a long time for anyone. It seems even longer to a refugee who can rarely carry on the normal activity that most of us need to help provide a sense of self-respect and even identity.

To look for solutions for long-stayers, it is best to go back to the classic solutions and see how they can most appropriately be applied.

Repatriation

A return home is normally considered the best solution for refugees. It has been possible many times over the last 40 years. Recently, however, there have been only limited possibilities for repatriation because most crises that have generated refugees have not yet ended and do not seem likely to end soon.

Repatriation is a difficult solution to implement when refugees return to a country or an area where the basic situation that may have led to exile has not changed, where the government they fled is still in power, or where some conflict is still in progress even if at a lower level of violence. Many refugees are afraid to return. The governments often do not want them back. As can be seen from the discussion of separate refugee situations, repatriation may often be controversial. Nonetheless, in many instances in Africa and Latin America when conditions at home have seemed better – albeit still uncertain – refugees have chosen repatriation in order to resume some semblance of normal life.

On the basis of these considerations, the possibilities for repatriation should not be neglected. The following guidelines appear to offer some hope of meeting refugee wishes for repatriation while assuring their safety:

- Repatriation should be encouraged wherever possible.
- The most basic condition is that repatriation must retain its entirely voluntary character, with some way to verify independently that the choice is truly a free one.
- There should also be an independent and fully adequate monitoring capacity in the country of repatriation whenever doubt exists.
- There should be some consultation between the High Commissioner and members of the Executive Committee or countries in the repatriation area to determine if diplomatic or other steps can be taken to help assure the safety of the repatriates.

Integration and Special Support
for Asylum Countries

Integration into the asylum country remains one of the best solutions, especially in Africa. The effectiveness of the set-

tlement concept must constantly be reviewed and improved, however. Settlements should be properly integrated
into the national environment and should offer refugees a
promising opportunity to earn and to contribute. The con-
struction of such settlements should be accelerated wherever possible and appropriate, in consultation with local development agencies and authorities as well as with the
refugees.

ICARA II gave birth to a successful concept but not to
a successful program. The program's momentum was un-
dercut at the outset by the necessary diversion of resources
to drought and famine relief. It is now clear, however, that
there was a fundamental flaw in the structure established
to administer the ICARA II program. The agencies that
have the greatest incentive to initiate projects do not have
the principal program responsibility, either at the national
or international level, and the agencies that have the principal program responsibility often have other priorities. The
African asylum governments are not proposing new projects because they are not certain that those projects will
call forth truly additional resources. Yet, until ICARA II functions properly, growing African concerns about the negative impact of a refugee presence can impede integration.

To give the ICARA II concept an opportunity to be
carried forward more effectively, the following steps should
be taken:

• The High Commissioner's budget should have a re-
volving fund between $1 million to $3 million to be used for
initial proposal, design, contracting, and fund-raising for
new projects and for up-dating earlier ones that might still
have merit.

• The ICARA II steering committee should become a
more flexible instrument, going beyond the original four
partners. All development agencies that are interested in
ICARA II and in managing programs should be invited to
join the committee or at least to attend meetings periodical-
ly. So should representatives of voluntary agencies.

- Agencies represented on that committee should meet on a regular schedule not only in the committee forum itself but in interested asylum countries.
- Efforts to involve voluntary agencies in the ICARA II concept and in specific projects should be intensified.
- Wherever possible, opportunities for private funding or at least participation should be offered.
- The African governments of asylum must make their own attitudes on the ICARA II concept and program clearly understood. Without their interest and support, it cannot and will not succeed.
- ICARA II projects should be more closely tied to actual refugee settlement, self-sufficiency, and income-generating projects, especially projects that can quickly benefit refugees as well as the local population and economy.

Resettlement

Resettlement is not generally considered an ideal refugee solution. Nonetheless, it has constituted the best available solution for Indochinese refugees and often serves for refugees from other countries, particularly for the professional classes. Most programs appear to be working properly. Preliminary indications are that most resettled refugees are doing reasonably well.

There remains, however, the long-standing problem of the refugees in Southeast Asia. Their numbers are below 140,000, less than 10 percent of those who originally fled Indochina.

Indochinese refugee resettlement has been an immense operation in scope, in numbers of persons moved, in common effort, and in common success. It has constituted one of the most generous achievements of this or any century. Now, however, stagnation has set in for most long-stayers. Moreover, some who are now fleeing Indochina are really migrants who want to join their families in the West, but by establishing refugee status they delay not only true refugees but also others who want to join their families. Another problem is that the Southeast Asian countries of first asylum, disturbed by these developments, are threatening to return true refugees as well as others if the West does not take all those in the camps. Yet Indochinese refugee resettlement cannot be permitted to end in what would be not only a failure of a program but a failure of international humanitarian will. It must be brought to a decent close.

• A renewed and coordinated effort should be made by all resettlement countries, working closely with the High Commissioner and with countries of first asylum, to find a solution for those persons who are still left in camps. The solution should either be resettlement or some other means that might be appropriate and acceptable to refugees, countries of asylum, and, if repatriation is involved, countries of origin.

• This should be done as a planned, coordinated program over several years, not as a haphazard series of separate decisions. No country should be asked to make this its exclusive effort. All countries with any past or present role in the program should be invited to participate.

• As was done in Europe in 1959–1960, the principle of camp clearance should be followed, with the remaining camp inhabitants that can be selected for resettlement duly apportioned among interested participating countries and moved within a definite time period. Even those who have been rejected must be reexamined in that spirit. It is not humane to deny resettlement to refugees and their families who have waited for almost 10 years, unless they are demonstrably criminals.

• To avoid inviting a renewed flow, a careful screening process should be announced, with known and agreed upon criteria for all new arrivals to qualify for refugee status. Those who fail to pass that process should be returned when a humane process can be negotiated, but they cannot expect resettlement.

• The camps whose locations have a magnet effect should be closed or moved. The operation should have lower costs and lower visibility. It must be made clear that the objective of the special camp clearance effort is to put an end to the camps, not to perpetuate them, even though it will be necessary to preserve some possibility for asylum to those in genuine need as is done for those who leave Eastern Europe.

• The prospect of returning refugees or asylum applicants to each of the countries of Indochina may appear inhumane, even impossible. It should not be done lightly. But repatriation by the asylum countries is becoming a genuine risk for long-stayers. It is better to warn potential new arrivals than to repatriate those who are already refugees.

• The ODP effort should be reinvigorated and if possible extended to Laos. It remains the most humane way to bring out refugees and their family members. It also could represent a way to expand legal emigration for people who would not qualify as refugees but want to join their families in the West. Negotiations should be continued and, if necessary put in the hands of a special senior envoy, speaking for all interested governments.

• Local integration for some groups should be seriously explored. Although it may not have been possible in the past, it could perhaps be brought about if it were part of an overall solution. Discussions on that possibility should be opened and funds made available.

For New Arrivals

Ultimately, any effort to solve the global refugee problem must attempt to address the intercontinental asylum seekers. The hardest element in this will be to help the true refugees, to reject the obviously false, and to find a fair solution for the humanitarian cases.

This problem cannot be solved in isolation. It must be addressed as part of the complex of new and tangled issues involving refugee protection, migration, foreign labor, and the relations between North and South. It is now physically, economically, and politically impossible for any part of the world to shut itself off. Any solution must be sought in that spirit, and in a spirit of humanitarianism.

Regionalization is a potentially dangerous concept. There cannot be two systems for refugee protection and care. One of the great achievements of the past several decades has been the integration of different elements of refugee law and of different practices and traditions into one global system of refugee protection and care. Those who have created and supported that system cannot benefit from its dissolution.

A solution must also be designed not just to react to the current problem but to function over the long term. If there is to be a new visa and immigration regime in Western Europe by 1992, the years between now and then should permit time to arrange a common policy and to coordinate appropriate elements of it with North American states.

Key elements of a policy should be the following:

• To reduce the large illegal and quasi-legal population that exists underground and that attracts others, amnesty should be offered to those who are living undocumented or under some variation of the "B" status in West European states.

• The utmost generosity should be shown to persons who qualify or appear to qualify as refugees on the basis of the 1951 convention, giving the benefit of the doubt wherever possible. They must continue to have a chance to state their case. They must not be prevented from entering a country or addressing authorized immigration officials.

• Rapid and absolute rejection should confront applicants who are clearly economic migrants disguised as refugees. Early return should be arranged. As Sadruddin Aga Khan has observed, "the right of asylum has been abused."[149] The status of refugee is a precious institution that has saved many lives and should not now be jeopardized by such abuse.

• For those who flee violence, temporary haven is a necessity – along with a common policy based on accurate information, careful coordination, and strict enforcement. Decisions should be made on the basis of European or Western-coordinated estimates of the situation, with information also from the countries of the region where the asylum seekers originate.

• When such applicants are admitted, it should be made clear that admission is not permanent, is subject to periodic review, and carries none of the rights of a convention refugee but represents an effort to help in an emergency. Refuge should be possible, but not attractive, and should be treated as a clearly temporary and minimally assisted situation.

• All affected asylum states should introduce simplified procedures, shorter processing times, and reinforced staff for evaluating applications and for enforcing decisions. The process should be improved, not closed off.

• A new and expanded structure of internal control should be introduced. Expanded employer sanctions, which (like amnesty) have been or are being tried with some effectiveness by various Western countries, could be included. The public will not allow governments to be generous if it believes they have lost control. That control must be reestablished.

• Higher levels of assistance should be provided to countries of first asylum. They should be offered refugee aid and economic assistance. Moreover, if they find themselves under pressure from countries of origin, especially neighboring countries, they should receive diplomatic and political support as well as immediate help in arranging the onward travel of those asylum seekers whose presence is particularly sensitive.

• A major resettlement program should be a part of any West European plan for a common visa and documentation regime. If the West European states by 1992 have, in effect, moved toward the "regionalization" that they claim to seek, using airlines to refuse access, no asylum seeker will be able to reach Western Europe except those who may enter from Eastern Europe and perhaps from the Middle East. Their situation will resemble that of the United States, Canada, and Australia. Those countries, however, maintain significant resettlement programs to relieve the pressure on countries of first asylum, and any European system should have such an element as well as the other recommendations suggested above.

• If these steps are not sufficiently implemented and coordinated, and if problems and controversies persist or are further exacerbated, the industrialized countries should create a special international commission of senior statesmen to propose common policies. Such a group could bring to this delicate and immensely complex humanitarian dilemma the kind of moral and political authority, and the kind of human understanding, that is essential to success.

Such measures may at first appear draconian, but they are not out of proportion to the need. A number of West European and North American states are already taking some of them in order to retain their ability to be selective in the face of the growing stream of intermingled migrants and refugees. It is important, however, for these actions to be taken in coordination and with a sense of ultimate purpose, so that in the process of implementation the West will not abandon the generous spirit that has for so long guided, and must continue to guide, its policies in this domain.

* * * *

Over the last several decades, refugee crises have erupted so quickly and on such a massive scale that conceptual changes had to be made under pressure and sometimes in haste. Nonetheless, a number of new concepts were introduced by the High Commissioners or by governments, acting in close coordination, and new levels of refugee protection and care have been reached and maintained. Those concepts and those efforts gained popular and political acceptance. They have constituted a real achievement that should be a source of pride to the persons, the private organizations, and the nations that have contributed so generously.

Now, as crises have multiplied and as many refugee situations remain unsolved, fresh ideas must be explored, discussed, and implemented. Moreover, the system must continue to function in a way that will garner international understanding and popular support.

The common objective should be to preserve the global structure of refugee protection and care, to help those who need help, to prevent abuse, and to bring refugee concepts and practices into a framework appropriate to our troubled times.

Notes

1. W. R. Smyser, "Refugees: A Never-Ending Story," *Foreign Affairs* (Fall, 1985), 166–167.

2. Gunther Beyer, "The Political Refugee 35 Years Later," Barry N. Stein and Sylvano M. Tomasi, eds., *Refugees Today*, Special Issue of *International Migration Review* (Spring–Summer, 1981), 28–30.

3. Louise W. Holborn, *Refugees: A Problem of our Time*, vol. 1 (Metuchen, N.J.: The Scarecrow Press, 1975), 5–7. For detailed discussion of the interwar refugee movement, see Mendel R. Marcus, *The Unwanted* (New York: Oxford University Press, 1985), 51–295, and Paul Frings, *Das Internationale Fluechtlingsproblem* (Frankfurt am Main: Verlag der Frankfurter Hefte, 1952), 15–56.

4. Neremiah Robinson, *Convention Relating to the Status of Refugees* (New York: Institute for Jewish Affairs, 1953), 2–3.

5. Ibid.

6. Holborn, *Refugees*, vol. 1, p. 24.

7. Ibid., 25–27.

8. For a full history of the International Refugee Organization, see Louise W. Holborn, *The International Refugee Organization* (London: Oxford University Press, 1956).

9. *Collection of International Instruments Concerning Refugees* (Geneva: United Nations High Commissioner for Refugees [UNHCR], 1979), 11.

10. James C. Hathaway, "The Evolution of Refugee Status in

International Law, 1920–1950," *International and Comparative Law Quarterly* (April, 1984), 379–380.

11. Much has been written about the 1951 convention and its specific provisions. Useful references include Holborn, *Refugees*, vol. 1, 158–173; Robinson, *Convention*, 9–180; and Guy Goodwin-Gill, *The Refugee in International Law* (Oxford: Clarendon Press, 1983), 149–164. For a full review of refugee law, see Atle Grahl-Madsen, *The Status of Refugees in International Law*, 2 vols. (Leiden: The Netherlands: A. W. Sijthoff, 1971).

12. Holborn, *Refugees*, vol. 1, pp. 177–182.

13. For the text of the protocol, see *Collection of International Instruments*, 40–44.

14. Holborn, *Refugees*, vol. 1, pp. 183–187.

15. L. G. Eriksson, G. Melander, and P. Nobel, *An Analysing Account of the Conference on the African Refugee Problem, Arusha, May 1979* (Uppsala, Sweden: Scandinavian Institute of African Studies, 1981), 9. For discussion of the effects of African nation-building on refugee creation, see Aristide R. Zolberg, "The Formation of new States as a Refugee-generating Process," Gilbert D. Loescher and John A. Scanlan, eds., *The Global Refugee Problem: U.S. and World Response*, special edition of *The Annals* (May, 1983), 24–38.

16. For the text of the OAU convention, see *Collection of International Instruments*, 193–200. For a general discussion of legal questions pertaining to African refugees, see Goeran Melander and Peter Nobel, eds., *African Refugees and the Law* (Uppsala, Sweden: The Scandinavian Institute of African Studies, 1978).

17. Resolution 319(IV), *United Nations Resolutions and Decisions relating to the Office of the United Nations High Commissioner for Refugees*, Fourth Edition, HCR/INF.48/Rev.3 (Geneva: UNHCR, 1984), I-2. (Hereinafter cited as *Resolutions*.)

18. Resolution 1167(XII), *Resolutions*, I-32.

19. James M. Read, *The United Nations and Refugees—Changing Concepts* (New York: Carnegie Endowment for International Peace, 1962), 31–32.

20. Resolution 1671(XVI), *Resolutions*, I-43.

21. Resolution 3143(XXVIII), *Resolutions*, I-75.

22. Resolutions 3455(XXX) and 31/55, *Resolutions*, I-83.

23. Resolution 32/67, *Resolutions*, I-88.

24. Resolutions 40/118/119/132/133/134/135, *Resolutions*, I-176–184.

25. For more precise readings on the legal and operational meaning of the convention definition, see *Handbook on Procedures and Criteria for Determining Refugee Status* (Geneva: UNHCR, 1979).

26. Ignatius Bau, *This Ground is Holy* (New York: Paulist Press, 1985), 124–157; Ghassan M. Arnaout, *L'Asile dans la Tradition Arabo-Islamique* (Geneva: International Institute of Humanitarian Law, 1986).

27. Text in *Collection of International Instruments*, 101. For discussion of this particular question and of national reluctance to grant an assured right of asylum, see Goodwin-Gill, *The Refugee in International Law*, 102–123; The Independent Commission on International Humanitarian Issues, *Refugees* (London: Zed Books, 1986), 31–42; Goeran Melander, "Refugees and International Cooperation," Stein and Thomasi, eds. *Refugees Today*, 35–38; Gilbert Jaeger, "Refugee Asylum: Policy and Legislative Developments," Ibid., 52–68; Dale Frederick Swartz, "First Asylum and Governance," Lydio F. Tomasi, ed., *In Defense of the Alien*, vol. V, (New York: Center for Migration Studies, 1983), 71–78; Joachim Henkel, "International Protection of Refugees," Ibid., 53–63.

28. Texts in *Collection of International Instruments*, 193–201, 264–267, 306.

29. *Collection of International Instruments*, 57–58.

30. Goodwin-Gill, *The Refugee in International Law*, 109–111.

31. Ibid., 119–121.

32. The statistics on the IRO discussion are drawn from Holborn, *The International Refugee Organization*, 122–126.

33. Holborn, *Refugees*, vol. 1, pp. 323–463.

34. Read, *The United Nations and Refugees*, 42–48, provides some examples of the levels of funding needed for various programs.

35. J. G. Van Heuven Goedhart, *Refugee Problems and their Solutions* (Geneva: UNHCR, 1955), 20.

36. *Resolutions*, I-29.

37. Statistics on the UNHCR annual assistance programs are drawn from the UNHCR's annual reports to the Executive Committee, entitled *UNHCR Activities financed by Voluntary Funds*, published as UN General Assembly documents in the A/AC.96 series. The final annual totals are drawn from the year after

the program is completed because the inherently unpredictable nature of refugee situations makes it impossible to estimate in advance what exact expenditures may be required for any given program year.

38. Resolution 35/41, *Resolutions*, I-104.

39. Resolution 35/183, *Resolutions*, I-115.

40. Resolution 39/106, *Resolutions*, I-162.

41. Resolution 40/135, *Resolutions*, I-183.

42. Resolution 40/117, *Resolutions*, I-174.

43. Resolution 41/124, *Resolutions adopted on the Reports of the Third Committee* (New York: UN General Assembly, n.d.), 359.

44. Resolution 41/122, *Resolutions adopted on the Reports of the Third Committee*, 355.

45. UNHCR, *UNHCR Activities Financed by Voluntary Funds*, Report Submitted to the UNHCR Executive Committee, October, 1986, A/AC.96/677 (Part I), 29.

46. Shelly Pitterman, "International Responses to Refugee Situations: the United Nations High Commissioner for Refugees," Elizabeth G. Ferris, ed., *Refugees and World Politics* (New York: Praeger, 1985), 44–49.

47. U.S. Committee for Refugees (USCR), *World Refugee Survey, 1986 in Review* (Washington, D.C.: USCR, 1987), 38.

48. Some of the legal issues involved in repatriation are discussed in Guy Goodwin-Gill, *Voluntary Repatriation: Legal and Policy Issues* (Geneva: UNHCR, 1986).

49. USCR, *Despite a Generous Spirit* (Washington, D.C.: USCR, 1986), 36–37.

50. Reports on the financing and execution of the program are contained in *UNHCR Activities financed by Voluntary Funds* for the years 1982 through 1985.

51. Barry N. Stein, "Durable Solutions for Developing Country Refugees," Dennis Gallagher, ed., *Refugees: Issues and Directions*, special issue of *International Migration Review* (Summer, 1986), 270–271.

52. Ibid.

53. For a general review of settlements in Africa and introduction to issues involved, see John R. Rogge, "Africa's Settlement Strategies," Ferris, ed., *Refugees and World Politics*, 168–186. For a general discussion of the difficulties of arranging

durable solutions in developing countries, see Stein, "Durable Solutions for Developing Country Refugees," 264–282.

54. USCR, *World Refugee Survey. 1986 in Review*, 40.

55. U.S. Coordinator for Refugee Affairs, *Proposed Refugee Admissions and Allocations for Fiscal Year 1987* (Washington, D.C.: U.S. Coordinator, 1986), 38.

56. For example, Part IV of Gallagher, ed., *Refugees*, 329–501; Julia Vadala Taft, "Time to refocus Refugee Resettlement Strategies," Tomasi, ed., *In Defense of the Alien*, 79–84; Paul J. Strand and Woodrow Jones, Jr., *Indochinese Refugees in the United States: Problems of Adaptation and Assimilation* (Durham, N.C.: Duke University Press, 1984); Scott Morgan and Elizabeth Colsen, eds., *People in Upheaval* (New York: Center for Migration Studies, 1987); James T. Fawcett and Benjamin V. Carino, eds., *Pacific Bridges* (New York: Center for Migration Studies, 1987); Diakonisches Werk der Evangelischen Kirche Deutschlands, *Integration der Indochina Fluechtlinge* (Stuttgart: Diakonie, 1980). A good summary review is by Susan S. Forbes, *Adaptation and Integration of Recent Refugees to the United States* (Washington, D.C.: Refugee Policy Group [RPG], 1985).

57. For an analysis of adjustment factors and potential study areas, see Barry N. Stein, "The Refugee Experience: Defining the Parameters of a Field of Study," Stein and Tomasi, eds., *Refugees Today*, 320–330, especially 325.

58. For the records of these discussions, see UNHCR documents entitled *Refugee Aid and Development* as of the following dates: September 12, 1983 (A/AC.96/627); December 21, 1983 (A/AC.96/635); August 28, 1984 (A/AC.96/645); August 26, 1985 (A/AC.96/662).

59. A study commissioned by the UNHCR and written by Susan Goodwillie is annex III to A/AC.96/627. Others are Charles B. Keely, *Global Refugee Policy: the Case for a Development-oriented Strategy* (New York: Population Council, 1981); Ernst E. Boesch and Armin M. F. Goldschmidt, eds., *Refugees and Development*, a paper based on an international conference organized by the Development Policy Forum of the German Foundation for International Development, DSE (Baden-Baden, Germany: Nomos Verlagsgesellschaft, 1983).

60. UNHCR Activities financed by Voluntary Funds, A/AC.96/677, 1986 (Part I), 11.

61. Read, *The United Nations and Refugees*, 8.

62. The expansion of the High Commissioner's mandate has never led to any role for UNHCR with the Palestinians. The reasons for this are reviewed in Independent Commission on International Humanitarian Issues, *Refugees*, 50.

63. For a summary review of the first 20 years of UNHCR activity, especially the expansion of its functions, see UNHCR, *A Mandate to Protect and Assist Refugees* (Geneva: UNHCR, 1971) and Sadruddin Aga Khan, "Lectures on Legal Problems Relating to Refugees and Displaced Persons," UNHCR Document HCR/155/60/76, August 4–6, 1976, pp. 46–57.

64. Best source for this expansion of the UNHCR are annual reports to the Executive Committee.

65. A summary history and description of the ICM, from which much of the following material on the organization is drawn, is contained in the following article written by its director, James L. Carlin, "The Intergovernmental Committee for Migration: Thirty-five Years of Assistance to Refugees and Migrants," *Australian Foreign Affairs Record* (May, 1986), 398–407.

66. Interview with Trevor Page, director, Emergency Service, World Food Program, *Refugees* (December, 1986), 15–16.

67. *UNHCR Activities financed by Voluntary Funds*, 1986, (Part 1), 20.

68. Ibid., 20–23.

69. Summary information on voluntary agency involvement in refugee work is contained in Robert F. Gorman, "Private Voluntary Agencies in Refugee Relief," Ferris, ed., *Refugees and World Politics*, 82–104; Leon Gordenker, "Refugees in Developing Countries and Transnational Organization," Loescher and Scanlan, eds., *The Global Refugee Problem*, 62–77; Edgar H. S. Chandler, *The High Tower of Refuge* (New York: Praeger, 1959), 249–260. For listings of voluntary agencies, see UNHCR, *Directory of Voluntary Organizations* (Geneva: UNHCR, 1982); International Council of Voluntary Agencies, *Timely Solutions: Voluntary Agencies and African Refugees* (Geneva: ICVA, 1984).

70. See USCR, *World Refugee Survey, 1986 in Review*, 40, for full listing.

71. Peter I. Rose, *Working with Refugees* (New York: Center for Migration Studies, 1986), 103–108, raises some of these issues in the context of their impact on present organizations and experience.

72. For more detailed current refugee statistics, one can consult UNHCR annual reports to the Executive Committee, the annual USCR *World Refugee Survey*, or the annual U.S. State Department *World Refugee Report*. Recent articles and books containing numerical data on world refugees are by Yefime Zarjevski, *Garder Vivant l'Espoir* (Lausanne, Switzerland: L'Age d'Homme, 1985); Gilbert D. Loescher with Ann Dull Loescher, *The World's Refugees: a Test of Humanity* (New York: Harcourt Brace Jovanovich, 1982); and Earl E. Huyck and Leon F. Bouvier, "The Demography of Refugees," Loescher and Scanlan, eds., *The Global Refugee Problem*, 39–61.

73. More has been written about Indochinese refugees than about any other single group. Some useful references are Georges Condominas and Richard Pottier, *Les Rèfugiés originaires de l'Asie du Sud-Est* (Paris: La Documentation Francaise, 1982); Bruce Grant, *The Boat People* (Harmondsworth, England: Penguin Books, 1979); Lesleyanne Hawthorne, *Refugee: the Vietnamese Experience* (Melbourne: Oxford University Press, 1982); Gilbert D. Loescher and John A. Scanlan, eds., *Calculated Kindness* (New York: Free Press, 1986), 102–169; William Shawcross, *The Quality of Mercy* (New York: Simon and Schuster, 1984); Elliott L. Tepper, ed., *Southeast Asian Exodus* (Ottawa: Canadian Asian Studies Association, 1980); USCR, *People on the Edge: Cambodians in Thailand* (Washington, D.C.: USCR, 1985); U.S. Department of State, *The Indochinese Refugee Situation*, Report to the Secretary of State by the Special Refugee Advisory Panel, August 12, 1981; and U.S. Department of State, *Report of the Indochinese Refugee Panel*, April, 1986; Astri Suhrke, "Indochinese Refugees: the Law and Politics of First Asylum," Loescher and Scanlan, eds., *The Global Refugee Problem*, 116–137.

74. *New York Times*, June 7, 1987.

75. *Refugees* (April 1987), 10.

76. Ibid., 11–13.

77. USCR, *In Harm's Way: Refugees from Laos* (Washington, D.C.: USCR, 1986).

78. *Report of the Indochinese Refugee Panel*, 25–27.

79. *Wall Street Journal*, October 13, 1986.

80. Zolberg, "The Formation of new States as a Refugee-generating Process," Loescher and Scanlan, eds., *The Global Refugee Problem*, 24–38.

81. Holborn, *Refugees*, vol. 2, p. 830.

82. For an extended discussion of these and other African refugee groups during the 1950s, 1960s, and early 1970s, see Holborn, *Refugees*, vol. 2, pp. 959–1396.

83. For text of 1967 Addis Ababa conferences communique, the precursor to the OAU convention, see Hugh C. Brooks and Yassin El-Ayouty, eds., *Refugees South of the Sahara* (Westport, Conn.: Negro Universities Press, 1970), 251–260.

84. Eriksson et al., *An Analysing Account*, contains a full report on the Arusha conference.

85. Independent Commission on International Humanitarian Issues, *Refugees*, 26.

86. UNHCR, *UNHCR Activities financed by Voluntary Funds*, 1980, pp. 58–65.

87. This conference and its sequel are covered in detail in Robert Gorman, *Coping with Africa's Refugee Burden: A Time for Solutions* (Dordrecht, The Netherlands: Martinus-Nijhoff, 1987).

88. Robert Chambers, "Hidden Losers? The Impact of Rural Refugees and Refugee Programs on Poorer Hosts," Gallagher, ed., *Refugees*, 245–263.

89. A good summary of African concerns is a statement by UN Undersecretary General for Special Political Questions Abdulrahim A. Farah, *Refugee Aid and Development* (Geneva: International Council of Voluntary Agencies [ICVA], 1985). A further analysis of the problem is D. Lance Clark and Barry N. Stein, *The Relationship between ICARA II and Refugee Aid and Development* (Washington, D.C.: RPG, 1984).

90. Martin Barber, *Voluntary Agency Perspectives on Refugee Aid and Development* (Geneva: ICVA, 1985)

91. Interview with Maxime-Léopold Zollner, *Refugees* (July 1986), 16–18.

92. *Refugees* (January, 1987), 17–18.

93. *Refugees* (December, 1986), 20.

94. *Refugees* (January, 1987), 19; USCR, *Shattered Land, Fragile Asylum* (Washington, D.C., USCR, 1986).

95. *New York Times*, February 10, 1987.

96. *Frankfurter Allgemeine*, December 17, 1986.

97. *Refugees* (January, 1987), 8–10.

98. *Times* (London), February 3, 1987.

99. U.S. Congress, House of Representatives, *Reports on Refugee Aid* (Washington, D.C.: GPO, 1981), 71–75; Said Azhar,

"Three Million uprooted Afghans in Pakistan," *Pakistan Horizon* (First Quarter, 1985), 60–68.

100. Ijaz Hussain, "Pakistan's International Law Practice on Afghan Refugees," *Pakistan Horizon* (First Quarter, 1985), 85–89.

101. A useful summary of general refugee issues in Pakistan is in USCR, *Afghan Refugees: Five Years later* (Washington, D.C.: USCR, 1985).

102. *New York Times*, April 10, 1987.

103. Little has been written about refugees in Iran. The best sources for information are following reports in the magazine *Refugees* (May, 1984), p. 11; (November, 1985), 19–21, 27, as well as in UNHCR's reports to the Executive Committee since 1983.

104. For texts of these conventions, see *Collection of International Instruments*, 247–273.

105. UNHCR, *Declaracion de Cartagena* (Geneva: UNHCR, 1984), 34.

106. *Refugees* (March, 1986), 5.

107. U.S. Department of State, *Report of the Cuban-Haitian Task Force*, November 1, 1980, pp. A–5 to A–18, gives background on the Cuban exodus. Selected articles on Cuban refugees appear in Carlos E. Cortes, ed., *Cuban Refugee Programs* (New York: Arno Press, 1980).

108. Ronald Copeland, "The Cuban Boatlift of 1980: Strategies in Federal Crisis Management," Loescher and Scanlan, eds., *The Global Refugee Problem*, 138–150.

109. *Refugees* (March, 1986), 38–39.

110. Ibid.

111. Ibid.; *Report of the Cuban-Haitian Task Force*, pp. A–18 to A–26; Naomi Flink Zucker, "The Haitians versus the United States: The Courts as last Resort," Loescher and Scanlan, eds., *The Global Refugee Problem*, 151–162.

112. These and immediately succeeding statistics are drawn from U.S. Congress, *Central American Refugees, Hearings before the Subcommittee on Census and Population of the Committee on Post Office and Civil Service*, House of Representatives (Washington, D.C.: GPO, 1985), 7–25.

113. Elizabeth G. Ferris, "Regional Responses to Central American Refugees," in Ferris, ed., *Refugees and World Politics*, 187–209.

114. These statistics are drawn from UNHCR reports to the Executive Committee and from the following issues of *Refugees*

magazine: (October 1985), 17–18; (January 1986), 14–16; (May 1986), 27–28; (July 1986), 19–30; (August 1986), 19–31; (October 1986), 19–30.

115. USCR, *World Refugee Survey, 1986 in Review*, 60.

116. *Le Monde*, International Edition, February 19–25, 1987.

117. Bau, *This Ground is Holy*.

118. USCR, *The Asylum Challenge to Western Nations* (Washington, D.C.: USCR, 1984), 13.

119. *New York Times*, August 16 and 20, 1985, and November 3, 1986.

120. Press release by the government of Canada, February 10, 1987.

121. A table reflecting these differences is carried in Michael S. Teitelbaum, *Latin Migration North* (New York: Council on Foreign Relations, 1985), 28.

122. *New York Times*, May 3, 1987.

123. Ibid., May 15, 1987.

124. For information on East European refugees, particularly during the early postwar years, see the following: Aaron Levenstein, *Escape to Freedom* (Westport, Conn.: Greenwood Press, 1983), 3–99; Marcus, *The Unwanted*; Malcolm J, Proudfoot, *European Refugees* (Evanston, Ill.: Northwestern University Press, 1956).

125. U.S. Department of State, *World Refugee Report, 1986* (Washington, D.C.: U.S. Department of State, 1986), 63–65.

126. UNHCR, *UNHCR Activities financed by Voluntary Funds*, 1986.

127. *Refugees* (December 1986), 22.

128. *New York Times*, January 11, 1987.

129. Ibid., March 8, 1987.

130. *Washington Post*, April 15, 1987.

131. *New York Times*, March 31, 1987.

132. This chapter on intercontinental refugees deals with a fast-moving situation and most sources, therefore, are from current magazines, particularly *Refugees*, and newspapers. Because the magazine and press articles often cover only particular countries and particular situations, whereas this chapter moves from country to country and sometimes combines common elements of the refugee story from several countries into one sentence, it is impossible to create endnotes in the usual manner because they

would duplicate each other and require constant cross-referencing. For those interested in further reading on the particular situations, the following constitute useful current references with more detail than can be presented in this chapter:

Asylum in Europe as a whole: Guy Goodwin-Gill, "International Law and the Detention of Refugees and Asylum-Seekers," Gallagher, ed., *Refugees*, 193-219; Goran Melander, "Responsibility for Examining an Asylum Request, Asylum Seekers vs. Quota Refugees," Ibid., 220-229; *Refugees* (May 1985), 5; (July 1985), 19-30; (December 1986), 22; *New York Times*, July 8, 1984; *Sunday Times* (London), April 29, 1984; *Guardian*, November 29, 1986, December 5, 1986. An excellent guide to asylum practices and procedures in European countries is *Asylum in Europe*, published by the European Consultation on Refugees and Exiles in 1983.

Austria: *Refugees* (December 1986), 9-12.

Canada: *Refugees* (April 1986), 39; (June 1986), 43; (February 1987), 17-43; (March 1987), 14; *Times* (London), February 27, 1987.

France: *Refugees* (May 1984), 29-32; (February 1985), 33-34; (March 1986), 13-14; (June 1986), 31-33; (November 1986), 42-43; (March 1987), 31-32.

Germany and West Berlin: Federal Republic of Germany, press release, January 7, 1987; *Refugees*, (March 1986), 39-40; (September 1986), 16; (October 1986), 32-34; *Frankfurter Allgemeine*, January 8, February 18, 19, 28, March 3, 7, April 3, 1987; *Der Spiegel* (December 15, 1986), 53-55; *Die Zeit*, February 6, 1987.

Great Britain: *Refugees* (November 1985), 43-44; (August 1986), 34-37; *Daily Mail*, February 18, 1987; *Independent*, February 18, 1987; *Neue Zuercher Zeitung*, March 5, 1987 (all dates for this newspaper given from the international edition); *Times* (London), February 18, 26, March 4, 1987.

Italy: *Refugees* (January 1984), 13-14.

Netherlands: *Refugees* (July 1986), 36-37.

Scandinavia: *Refugees* (June 1984), 21-22; (January 1985), 39; (February 1986), 19-33.

Switzerland: *Refugees* (February 1984), 31-33; (October 1984), 38-39; (June 1985), 16-17; (August 1985), 42-43; (January 1986), 12-13; *Frankfurter Allgemeine*, March 28, 1987; *Neue*

Zuercher Zeitung, January 24, 30, 31, February 4, 8–9, 25, March 22–23, April 3, 1987; *New York Times*, April 6, 1987.

133. *Collection of International Instruments*, 304.

134. *Collection of International Instruments*, 305.

135. Mark J. Miller, *Employer Sanctions in Western Europe* (New York: Center for Migration Studies, 1987), 32, 42.

136. *Sunday Times* (London), March 15, 1987.

137. *Frankfurter Allgemeine Zeitung*, March 7, 1987.

138. *Refugees* (July 1985), 19–29.

139. The High Commissioner's speech to the Executive Committee, October 6, 1986, p. 6.

140. Joyce Pearce Memorial Lecture, Oxford University, October 29, 1986, p. 6.

141. *Neue Zuercher Zeitung*, February 13 and 14, 1987; *Journal de Genève*, February 14, 1987; *Tribune de Genève*, February 28, 1987.

142. Melander, "Refugees and International Cooperation."

143. *Refugees* (May 1984), 20.

144. *Refugees* (April 1984), 5; (May 1984), 20–28.

145. Loescher and Scanlan, eds., *Calculated Kindness*.

146. Goodwin-Gill, "International Law and the Detention of Refugees and Asylum-Seekers," Gallagher, ed., *Refugees*, 193–219; Conclusions on International Protection Adopted by the Executive Committee at its 28th Session, UN A/32/12/Add. 1, October, 1977.

147. Sadruddin Aga Khan, Special Rapporteur, "Study on Human Rights and Massive Exoduses," Commissioner on Human Rights, UN Economic and Social Council, December 31, 1981, E/CN.4/1503.

148. Note by the UN secretary general, *International Cooperation to Avert New Flows of Refugees*, A/41/324, May 13, 1986; UN General Assembly Resolution, same subject, A/RES/41/70, December 11, 1986.

149. Sadruddin, "Study on Human Rights and Massive Exoduses," 41.

Index